Cane Ridge

America's Pentecost

PAUL K. CONKIN

THE UNIVERSITY OF WISCONSIN PRESS

The University of Wisconsin Press
114 North Murray Street
Madison, Wisconsin 53715

3 Henrietta Street
London WC2E 8LU, England

5   4   3   2   1

Printed in the United States of America

Library of Congress Cataloging-in-Publication Data

Conkin, Paul Keith.
Cane Ridge: America's Pentecost / Paul K. Conkin.
198 pp.   cm. — (The Curti lectures: 1989)
Includes index. 1. Cane Ridge Revival (1801: Bourbon County, Ky.)
2. Revivals—Kentucky—Bourbon County—History—19th century.
3. Bourbon County (Ky.)—Church history—19th century.
I. Title. II. Series.
BV3774.K4C65   1990
269'.24'09769423—dc20
ISBN 0-299-12720-6   90-50081
ISBN 0-299-12724-9 (pbk.)   CIP

THE CURTI LECTURES

The University of Wisconsin-Madison
1989

To honor the distinguished historian Merle Curti,
lectures in social and intellectual history
were inaugurated in 1976 under the sponsorship of the
University of Wisconsin Foundation and the
Department of History of the University of Wisconsin-Madison.

PUBLISHED BY THE UNIVERSITY OF WISCONSIN PRESS

Christopher Hill, *Some Intellectual Consequences of the
English Revolution* (1980)

Carlo M. Cipolla, *Fighting the Plague in
Seventeenth-Century Italy* (1981)

James Willard Hurst, *Law and Markets in United States History:
Different Modes of Bargaining among Interests* (1982)

Gordon A. Craig, *The End of Prussia* (1984)

Michael Kammen, *Spheres of Liberty: Changing Perceptions of Liberty in
American Culture* (1986)

Contents

Illustrations

Preface and Acknowledgments

For a long time, I have wondered what really happened at
Cane Ridge in 1801. Like Jonathan Edwards's revival in Northampton in 1734, the Cane Ridge revival has become a legendary event in American history. The accounts of what happened, although numerous, seemed to me both variant and
elusive. The more I read about Cane Ridge the more I wanted
answers to several questions about it. I also sensed a good
story, one both dramatic and significant. I yearned to tell it.
An invitation to present the Curti Lectures at the University of
Wisconsin offered me the ideal opportunity. This small book
is the text, not of the necessarily more abridged lectures, but
of the fuller story from which I derived the lectures.

Every historical subject presents its own unique challenges
and hazards. The great Cane Ridge meeting of 1801 was, in
one sense, a very local event. But in trying to understand it, I
kept moving out to broader and broader issues. The context
turned out to be anything but local, which may be true for any
human event when one seeks the fullest undertanding. Also,
the influence of Cane Ridge soon appeared much greater
than I had ever imagined. Thus, very local events took on
almost cosmic significance. But the event, rooted in time and
place, demanded its due. Thus, this book has to measure up
to two standards. As very local history, it has to be accurate
about even minutiae—the exact date or even hour of each

event, the correct physical setting, the correct order of events, who did what and when, even details about the weather. At the other extreme, it must probe all the subtleties of ancient beliefs affirmed by the various persons at Cane Ridge and identify the continuities reflected in the traditional rituals that they reenacted.

Acknowledgments are in order. One debt is to Merle Curti, friend and former colleague, whose gifts and personal advice enabled the University of Wisconsin to establish the Curti Lectures. At the age of ninety-one, he attended each of my three lectures and was soon as intellectually involved with their content as anyone in the audience. To him, and to others of my former colleagues at the University of Wisconsin, I offer thanks not only for this opportunity but for so many treasured memories that stretch back well over twenty years.

As an undergraduate student at Vanderbilt, Ted Ownby chose to complete an excellent bachelor's thesis on the Logan County revivals. His work stimulated my growing interest in Cane Ridge, and his findings helped guide my own very brief treatment of events in Logan County. As soon as I began work on Cane Ridge, I realized that I followed very closely in the footsteps of John B. Boles, who wrote not only a much esteemed history of the Great Revival in the South, but also a brief volume on Christianity in early Kentucky. His books became my primary guide to bibliography, and offered the broader background to the more focused story I wished to tell. I ended up with some very different perspectives on Cane Ridge, but ones that I believe complement rather than contradict Boles's conclusions. I soon realized the futility of citing his works in what would have been almost endless notes, for on the main chronology of events I often followed his lead, albeit with a perhaps perverse eye for very different details. Without his earlier work, my research would have been twice as difficult, perhaps at some points impossible.

After this book was at press, I learned about an excellent Ph.D. dissertation (University of Chicago, 1988) by Ellen T.

Eslinger, "The Great Revival in Bourbon County, Kentucky." It offers an almost definitive account of the social, political, and economic setting for the revival of 1801, and in its description of Cane Ridge, provides a useful complement to my doctrinal and institutional perspective.

The research for this book did not involve extensive archival work. I appreciate the courtesy shown my by the staff of the Kentucky Museum at Western Kentucky University, the Library of the University of Kentucky at Lexington, the Manuscripts Division of the Kentucky Historical Society, the State Historical Society of Wisconsin, and the Disciples of Christ Historical Society. Franklin R. McGuire, curator of the Old Cane Ridge Meeting House, was a very helpful and informative host during my two-day visit to that shrine. I was able to complete the final revisions and ready this manuscript for publication during a sabbatical leave made possible by Vanderbilt University and by a University Fellowship granted by the National Endowment for the Humanities.

Cane Ridge

Doctrines and Institutions

Cane Ridge has a special, epochal position in American religious history. From August 6 through 12, 1801, in the first summer of a new century, thousands of people gathered in and around the small Cane Ridge meetinghouse in Bourbon County in central Kentucky to prepare for and then celebrate the Lord's Supper. Never before in America had so many people attended this type of sacramental occasion. Never before had such a diversity of seizures or "physical exercises" affected, or afflicted, so many people. The Cane Ridge sacrament has become a legendary event, the clearest approximation to an American Pentecost, prelude to a Christian century. It arguably remains the most important religious gathering in all of American history, both for what it symbolized and for the effects that flowed from it.

Institutionally, in the intent of its organizers, Cane Ridge was a great Presbyterian communion service. For unclear reasons, most historians have ignored or slighted this simple, obvious fact, and as a result have crucially distorted what happened. In almost every detail, the communion service at Cane Ridge conformed to a two-centuries-old, highly ritualized sacramental tradition that distinguished Scottish and Ulster Presbyterianism from other Reformed confessions. In fact, Cane Ridge was not as large, not as lengthy, and probably not as boisterous as four or five famous communions of the same type that occurred in southwest Scotland and in Ulster during the seventeenth and eighteenth centuries. But—and this is critically important—it was not only the largest such communion service in the New World, but in many respects it presaged the end of that tradition. An ethnic tradition, by 1800 more lovingly preserved by Scotch-Irish Presbyterians in America than back in Ulster and Scotland, would soon expire. Embryonic at Cane Ridge were new institutions—organized camp meetings and nonsacramental revival meetings in churches.

The events at Cane Ridge helped splinter Presbyterians in Kentucky and Tennessee, temporarily halting the local growth of the denomination. In the controversies that followed the great communion lay the seeds of the later Cumberland Presbyterian church and also the Restoration or Christian Movement, first led by the host minister at Cane Ridge, Barton Warren Stone. The extremes of ecstasy also helped prepare the way for successful Shaker missionary efforts in Kentucky and Ohio.

Fully to understand Cane Ridge, one needs to move from a class—religion—to several subclasses—from Semitic religions to Christianity to Reformed Christianity to Scottish Presbyterianism, or from a phenomenon almost as inclusive as humanity itself to a relatively small branch of the Western church. Unfortunately, no firm semantic conventions govern the use of the ambiguous word *religion.* Thus I offer a simple way of classifying religions—one that descriptively involves beliefs, the quality of experience, rituals, and moral codes— that teleologically involves enlightenment or wisdom, ecstasy, worldly success, and salvation or life after death. In this taxonomy, Christianity is distinctive in its combined emphasis on correct belief and on salvation. It is, in other words, the prototypical doctrinal and salvationist religion. It subordinates, but does not exclude, characteristics and goals that are more prominent in other religions, such as enlightenment in Hinduism and Buddhism, rituals and moral codes in Judaism and Islam, and ecstasy in several African religions. These elemental distinctions help clarify the centrality of doctrines of salvation in the history of Christianity. They are critical to understanding not only Cane Ridge, but all types of evangelical Christianity in nineteenth-century America.

At its most fundamental level, Christianity shares with Judaism and Islam several basic assumptions. Early Christian intellectuals such as Paul lived in the shadow of these assumptions, could scarcely doubt them, even though Paul himself was a Hellenistic, even Hellenized, Jew. These assumptions include a form of theism—ultimate reality is unified, person-like, and usually masculine. They involve a cosmology—the one god created the heavens and the earth and all life, including human beings, with their distinctive ability to think and plan, and thus their unique moral accountability. They involve history—all events fulfill a divine plan, a providential design and purpose. They involve divine revelation—the creator god reveals his will to humans, his demands on them for obedience and faithfulness. They include redemptive promises. Those who willingly or lovingly obey such a god will receive great rewards. Finally, in late Judaism, in Christianity, in Islam, they involve some form of life beyond physical death. Either through the survival of an immortal spirit or mind, or by an eventual return to life of the resurrected self, or some combination of both, those in the god's favor will enjoy a perfected existence, one almost always defined as the absence, or the very opposite of, all the afflictions suffered in earthy life. Those out of the god's favor face either a second death after the resurrection or, if they are immortal, eternal spiritual torment.

This sketch is all drastically oversimplified. But it is often instructive, in our age, to confront, in such a stark outline, the guiding assumptions of all the Semitic religions, assumptions that have shaped so much of Western and Islamic civilization. Of course, every one of these core beliefs invites, indeed has received, myriad embellishments and interpretations. These elaborations developed, not usually as axiomatic affirmations, but as the inner logic of a series of dramatic narratives. They grew directly out of human experience.

Christianity developed out of a new set of narratives—those about Jesus of Nazareth. These narratives soon supported a critical, transforming overlay on late Second Temple and early rabbinic Judaism. The complex, not always consistent stories about Jesus—about his teaching, his miracles, his death, and his resurrection—allowed almost endless refinements and elaborations. Emerging Christianity was soon marred, or enriched, by internal divisions. Jewish Christian corporealists and moralists stood at an opposite pole from mystical and antinomian Gnostics. In between were the varied and always syncretistic traditions that matured in the six or seven major, so-called orthodox churches.

It is a long way from Christian beginnings to the Cane Ridge revival. Yet Cane Ridge makes sense only as a climactic outcropping of one major stream within Christianity that was tied to a particular conception of salvation first introduced by Paul and most consistently developed in his Letter to the Romans. It soon faced modifications in the growing Roman Catholic church. The two great sixteenth-century reformers, Luther and Calvin, both re-embraced an unusually pure and rigorous version of the Pauline scheme of salvation and tried to reform the Western church so as to give it a deserved centrality. They could not move the larger church far enough and thus separated from Rome, despite the preponderance of shared doctrines. The Catholic church in a sense reformed itself in the wake of such open rebellion and, in the process, moved even further from the Pauline scheme that Luther found, like seams of gold, within the earlier history of the church. In the dialectic of division, some of the disciples of Luther and Calvin, in their effort to flee as far as possible from Rome, stripped Christianity down toward its bare essentials, with the Pauline scheme of salvation towering above and shaping all else. Scottish and Irish Presbyterians became perfect exemplars of such a lean and hard reformed faith.

Back to the origins of this scheme. Paul is much too complex a person to characterize here. I want to focus only on his new plan of salvation, one so stripped of narrowly Jewish content, so transcultural, as to be appealing, he hoped, both to fellow Jews and to Gentiles. Paul became, in his own estimate, the apostle to the Gentiles. This mission dated from his supernatural confrontation with the risen Messiah in an explosive conversion experience. He soon became a psychologically penetrating critic of any legalistic, moralistic, or ritualistic approach to salvation, and more specifically a critic of the themes of law, obedience, and personal holiness he knew so well within his own pharisaic Judaism. The rules were sublime, the standard appropriately high. But no one could fully obey. Holiness was an impossible standard for egotistic, prideful humans. Only an outward, behavioral conformity was possible, and this veneer, by conventional standards, too often counted as righteousness. Thus the high moral demands of Judaism and the rituals of presentability or holiness became, to the sensitive, overly conscientious Paul, a burden, even a form of slavery. Always the law, duty, and inescapable guilt, the more so as the Jewish people comprehended more laws and their subtle demands, or as they looked more searchingly for the motives that guided their conduct. The law indicts or convicts but cannot liberate. Paul wanted to be free. He wanted to feel justified before his lofty, cosmic, all-powerful God, and this in spite of his inability to be holy. He wanted a new hope, a new approach to God and salvation, and he believed he found it in Jesus the risen Messiah or, in the Greek language, the Christ.

Paul added the first known coherent doctrinal overlay to the life and teachings of Jesus, which we may know better than Paul, who died before anyone had written one of the surviving Gospels. For Paul, the Christ opened the way to salvation based on trust and love, not legal obedience. Jesus, by his death, made such salvation possible. No one outside the Jewish sacrificial tradition, or without Paul's moral seriousness, could understand this point, which was central to the new religion. For such was the standard of purity required by the awesome justice of God that only perfect righteousness could make a person acceptable. Jesus was perfect, the special son of God. In the Jewish tradition of sacrificial offerings on behalf of purity, only his death could be a fully sufficient or atoning sacrifice. It alone could satisfy a divine standard of justice.

This atonement clarifies the terms of human salvation. The inordinate and egotistic nature of human beings does not allow them to meet the divine standard. Attempts to do so lead only to frustration. But Jesus gave new meaning to the old Jewish commandment to love God with all one's heart and mind and soul. Paul stripped this commandment of a purely legal meaning. People gained salvation, which to him meant not only a liberated and fulfilling life here but eternal life, by means of belief, trust, and love, or what he called faith. In a sense this scheme sounds easy. But that is the wrong term. It mistakenly assumes choice. Trust and love are never matters of choice; they command choice. If one loves the Christ, and through him God the Father, then one is reconciled, virtually assimilated, to the Christ. His righteousness becomes, vicariously, one's own.

How attain this love? What can one do? Again, the questions rest on mistaken premises—that love is chosen, worked for, earned. Paul knew better. He had met Jesus on the road to Damascus. In the fullest sense he had confronted the Christ, become acquainted with him. He was overwhelmed, lifted, he said in a contemporary astrological reference, into the third heaven. Anyone who met, who really knew, the Christ would love him. For such a person the beauty of the Christ is irresistible. This love, parent to all manner of choices, fount of intense affections, is a gift. And those who experience the transforming effects of such love, who gain a new repertoire of likes and dislikes, are really new persons. Reborn. As at their first birth, they cannot choose such a transformation. They can only be thankful for it and appropriately respond in joyous obedience.

Salvation is thus a gift, a matter of grace. Paul, always aware of his situation within the overweening providence of a cosmic deity, had to stop at this point and make the correct causal judgment. God selects us. His spirit illuminates us, opens our eyes to him or to the Christ. Unless he chooses us, elects us, salvation is impossible. And as an empirical fact, God has not chosen all for salvation. None deserve it, of course. His undeserved mercy is selective, conditional. For purposes unfathomable to human beings, he temporarily blinded the eyes of most Jews, made flawed vessels as well as perfect ones. Add some jargon, some philosophical distinctions, and what arises is such doctrines as omnipotence and predestination, labels that confuse more than they clarify. Skip ahead fifteen hundred years and one has the central doctrines of Reformed Christianity, or what some even yet call Calvinism.

Paul talked of a new Christian freedom, but this meant no license. It actually entailed a higher moral standard, one tied to the heart, to inward motives, much more than to external codes. Thus Paul became a staunch and moralistic churchman, participating in largely Gentile Christian communities, some organized before his conversion, and in churches that had already developed a rich liturgical life. He also celebrated the two sacraments of the early church, baptism and communion, and knew that salvation was logically inconceivable or impossible apart from the worship and sacraments of such Christian communities. He cherished the legendary day of Pentecost, when the divine Spirit came to Jesus' immediate disciples and gave them a new power and wonderful new gifts or blessings. In response, the original Christians broke out in ecstatic utterances. Paul himself knew the ecstasy produced by the Spirit, and at times established his credentials among Gentile Christians by his ecstatic speech. The gifts of the Spirit were also necessary for salvation, but like church membership, good deeds, or participation in the sacraments, they were logically, not causally, necessary. Each is inseparably linked to faith, but as a corollary of faith and not its cause. Each is meaningless or impossible apart from love, which is the all-important gift of the Spirit.

Luther and Calvin, in their attempt to reclaim this Pauline legacy, believed it had become all but lost in the corruptions that beset the Church of Rome. Sacramental obedience and priestly mediation had replaced, or at least obscured, faith as the sole causal condition of salvation. Infant baptism, when conceived as a remitting ordinance, had given almost everyone a false sense of ultimate security and lessened the import of human depravity. The doctrine of purgatory, tied to the confessional role of priests, kept people in a constant state of anxiety and fear, unsure of their ultimate fate. Numerous human-derived, often pagan practices distorted public worship, or deprived Christians of the consolation of the word of God as given in the scriptures. In spite of this, Luther and Calvin knew that people of faith remained in this sullied church. They also found most of their own intellectual weapons within its history. On the most basic issues—the nature of the Trinity, the human and divine traits in the Christ, limited atonement, justification of an ordained clergy and church order, basic creeds and confessions, the proper response to early heresies—they adhered to the Roman tradition. They were much closer to the old church than to several radical sects—free-will, separatist, legalistic Brethren or Anabaptists, or experiential spiritualists or enthusiasts such as the later Quakers.

A final doctrinal distinction needs to be made. The Pauline scheme of salvation remained central to all early Lutheran, Reformed, and Anglican churches. The sacraments in themselves were not saving ordinances. Faith alone was causally necessary for salvation, a faith engendered by an understanding of the Word of God as clarified by the Holy Spirit. This conception of salvation was, for Luther and Calvin, definitive of evangelical Christianity. Lutheran confessions, in particular, often incorporated the word *evangelical* in their titles. But by the eighteenth century the word increasingly designated an emphasis within Reformed churches on a crisis conversion, which meant an arduous and often extended rebirth experience, and on an affecting or experiential devotional life. This religion of the "twice-born"—to use William James's apt label—and of a warm spirituality contrasted with a more gradual, instructed, or ritualized path to church membership (the catechism and confirmation) and a less affectionate, less experiential, and more moralistic conception of discipleship.

These are illustrative polarities only, for few people moved to either extreme. Scottish Presbyterians tried to maintain a healthy middle road between the extremes. Early Methodists clearly moved far toward the twice-born or spiritual pole, while liberal or latitudinarian or rationalistic Presbyterians and Anglicans moved toward the once-born pole. My point is this—to make sense of Cane Ridge, or other great revivals in the early nineteenth century, one has to understand that the ministers who preached, and the lay people who responded, were already evangelicals in this new sense of the label. They knew that to become a Christian a person had to endure an arduous conversion, experience the depths of human despair and desolation, in order to gain a joy and happiness that approached beatitude.

Now to institutions. The various national Lutheran and Reformed churches all shared basic doctrines. Only relatively minor issues of belief distinguished each Lutheran or Calvinist confession. But practices soon varied. The original reformed churches—as in Lutheran Germany or Huguenot France—remained relatively formal or liturgical in worship. So did much of the English church, whose formal doctrines were soon thoroughly Calvinist. But more zealous reformers, particularly in England and Scotland, soon tried to expunge almost all human-derived elements of worship, moving back to the simple forms of the New Testament church as described in Acts. They valued plain worship services in simple meetinghouses, with scriptural teaching or sermons at the center of Sunday worship, supplemented by little more than scripture reading, public prayers, and psalm singing. In polity, the major reformed traditions varied, from a fully episcopal system in the English church and in Swedish Lutheranism to the predominating republican or presbyterial systems to radical congregationalism among some English Puritans and Calvinist Baptists.

As intended by its organizers, Cane Ridge reflected only one Reformed tradition—that of Scotland. I cannot here recount the complicated events of the Scottish Reformation, or clarify the many schisms within the resulting Scottish church. These are legendary. Small reform efforts in Scotland preceded Luther's protest and flowered into open but unsuccessful rebellion, with some exemplary martyrs, as early as 1547. At this point, a zealous young priest, John Knox, was able to leave prison and seek refuge, first in England, then on the Continent, where he eventually served as a pastoral colleague of John Calvin in Geneva. He already shared the doctrinal outlook of Luther and Calvin, but became enamored of the polity and the techniques of church discipline followed in Geneva. In the midst of a political civil war and a growing ascendancy of Protestant lords, Knox returned to Scotland by invitation at the end of 1559 to lead the Protestant cause. In 1560 the Scottish Parliament repudiated all lingering forms of the papal religion and approved a Protestant Confession, book of discipline, and the first meeting of a General Assembly of the Scottish church. Eventually, only the intervention of Queen Elizabeth of England, and the deposition of Mary, Queen of Scots, saved this reformation.

But this is only the opening of a complicated story. For over a hundred years the more rigorous Scottish Protestants struggled, with only one brief period of complete success, to escape prelacy and to institute a fully presbyterial polity. Even more than Calvin in Geneva, they tried to persuade, and at times openly defied, recalcitrant magistrates. The one brief interlude of success followed a dark period of high church persecution under the joint monarch, Charles Stuart. The Long Parliament embraced a presbyterial polity for England in 1642 and approved a Solemn League and Covenant that united the English and Scottish churches. In 1643 it convened an assembly of English divines (with Scottish observers) at Westminster, which, over the next four years, completed a new Confession, one as rigorously Reformed or Calvinist in doctrine as the earlier one drafted at Dort by the most orthodox churchmen in Holland. It also drafted a Larger and a Shorter Catechism, or a series of questions and answers that amplified the doctrines in the more formal Confession. These catechisms served as instructional manuals for almost all lay people in the Presbyterian church, and for children provided the instruction that led to confirmation and admission to the communion table. On only one issue—the mode of celebration of communion—did the Scottish observers continually disagree with their English Puritan colleagues. The Covenant and Confession became the golden reference points of the Scottish church, but the days of glory were brief, to be followed by divisions under Cromwell and the restoration of prelacy under Charles II.[1]

Before clarifying the central institutions of Scottish Presbyterianism, I should note the history of an Irish offshoot—the Presbyterian church of Ulster. It was by way of Ulster, much more frequently than Scotland, that Scottish Presbyterianism came to America. After brutal military campaigns, England gained control of the northern counties of Ireland by 1603. By that date, two Scottish lords had begun to establish Scottish tenants on new estates in Ulster. In 1607 James I offered

1. This brief survey of events in Scotland is almost general knowledge, and is documented in dozens of books on Presbyterian history. The Westminster Confession and the two catechisms still serve as definitive doctrinal statements in several branches of Presbyterianism, and as the most traditional of several accepted confessions in others. In 1729, the first American synod, that of Philadelphia, adopted both the Confession and the catechisms. Only after the Revolution, in 1787, did the newly organized Presbyterian Church in the United States of America make slight amendments in the chapters relating to church and state. Smaller seceder or reformed Presbyterian bodies did not accept these changes.

major incentives to other English or Scottish planters, who gained much of the land in Ulster under a form of feudal tenure. These planters in turn welcomed, with lower rents and no feudal obligations, leasehold farmers, most of whom came from the nearby southwest of Scotland (County Galloway in particular), where land was poor and rents high. These were mostly Presbyterians, but for a time they were unable to establish congregations. But to their good fortune, a handful of Presbyterian ministers from just across the North Channel refused to accept the role of bishops in Scotland and fled to Ulster after 1613, there to establish new Presbyterian congregations.[2]

In Ireland, as in Scotland, early Presbyterian success only began a century of strife and confusion. Irish Presbyterians never gained the status of an established church, but instead existed by suffrage under an often struggling Anglican establishment in a largely Catholic country. Under Archbishop Laud, and just after a period of stirring revivals, the Presbyterian ministers suffered such persecutions as to force them to flee back to Scotland. In 1642, with the Long Parliament ascendant in England, Presbyterian clergymen came back to Ulster with English troops and established the first informal presbytery. Under the Stuart Restoration, and even under William and Mary, Irish Presbyterians suffered numerous disabilities, but managed not only to survive but to grow, often through informal modes of evading the rules of the established church. The disabilities continued into the eigthteenth century. The much resented Test Act of 1704 had some small effect on the waves of Scotch-Irish emigration to the American colonies, although economic distress, crop failures, higher rents, and effective promotion of America best explain the largest exodus yet of Europeans to America.[3]

2. James G. Leyburn, *The Scotch-Irish: A Social History* (Chapel Hill: University of North Carolina Press, 1962), 83–98.
3. Peter Brooke, *Ulster Presbyterianism: The Historical Perspective, 1610–1970* (New York: St. Martins, 1987), 2–42.

Scottish and Irish ministers waited for over a century to secure the desired presbyterial polity. They were thus unable to gain a functional separation of church and state, or a fully self-governing church of a republican form. Governmental mandates limited the authority of local presbyteries, made up of delegates from individual congregations, and of the regional synods and, in Scotland, of the national General Assembly. But through most of the period after 1560, Presbyterians were able to maintain a local church order patterned on that of Geneva. With limited success, congregations asserted their right to call their own ministers. Local congregations were able at least to resist, or at times to make life miserable for clergymen chosen by landlords or by bishops. In the congregation, an order of deacons cared for worldly concerns. Elected lay elders (called ruling elders) joined with the teaching elder or minister to make up the main legislative and judicial body, the Session (called the Consistory in Geneva). Presbyterians recognized only two orders. Churchmen with special administrative duties might be called bishops, but they were otherwise the religious equals of other ministers or of teaching doctors in the universities. As late as the nineteenth century, Presbyterians in America still referred in ordination ceremonies to all their ministers as bishops, a title equivalent to presbyter or priest.

At the heart of the Geneva system was church discipline— the constant monitoring of lay belief and behavior. This made the Session a type of perennial grand jury and trial court. Its purpose was to nurture the faithful, bring to repentance the sinful, and use its powers to expel members so as to protect the integrity of the communion service. From the beginning, Presbyterians demanded a literate membership, and both parents and preachers accepted an obligation to develop local schools to educate a population largely illiterate before the reformation of the church. Presbyterians also set possibly the highest professional standards for their clergy in all Christendom. To become an ordained minister, one had to face more hurdles than a doctoral candidate does today. Candidates had to testify to a divine calling and to their own experimental faith, to present university credentials or else pass examinations on classical learning and scriptural understanding, and finally to complete an extensive trial period or internship. Presbyterian moral reform, and almost universal education, helped account for Scotland's transition, in only two hundred years, from one of the most poor and backward areas of Europe into one of the most prosperous and enlightened.

The Scottish church soon became most distinctive among Reformed bodies for its communion service. This service, much more than their polity or order of worship on Sunday, distinguished Scottish Presbyterians from English Puritans. In Scotland, the mode of administering the Lord's Supper became the most powerful symbol of Protestant-Catholic differences. The Protestants emphatically outlawed the Catholic Mass, and in particular rejected high masses on special holy days, such as Easter or the festival of Corpus Christi. Presbyterians tried to go back to the New Testament, to follow the earliest record of the Lord's Supper as celebrated at Corinth under the ministry of Paul. They therefore served the wine and bread on long tables set up in the aisles of the church and covered with white linen tablecloths and communion napkins. Communicants came forward to take seats for the supper (they were most horrified at kneeling). If the assemblage was large the tables might fill ten times, and a communion service, of logistic necessity, would take most of Sunday. The ministers gave the institution (a survey of the origins and purpose of the sacrament) and blessed the elements, but then took a seat with the elders at the head of the table. The ministers, elders, and lay people next passed around and partook of the platters of bread and the flagons or cups of wine, and after a prayer returned to their pews. The quantities of wine and bread were not mere tokens, but approximations of those consumed in an actual meal. Each seating repeated this procedure, except of course that the presiding minister ate and drank only once. Soon, in the typical joint communion services, different ministers presided at different tables. This was exactly the same type of communion that took place at Cane Ridge on August 8, 1801.[4]

Equally significant was the gradual expansion of this simple communion service into a three- to five-day affair. The patterns of development are not always clear, lost in the records of local parishes. Even by 1600 a few powerful ministers had elevated the communion service into the most intense, emotional occasion within the church. From the beginning the Scottish communion involved long preparatory sermons. It soon included not only instructions about the significance of the service, but careful warnings, often tied to specific commandments, about the dire consequences of coming to the table unprepared, without proper motives and a pure heart. This preparation came to be known as the "fencing of the table."

Scottish Presbyterians, like everyone within the Calvinist tradition, believed in the doctrine of spiritual presence. In the communion, the elements did not miraculously become the blood and body of the Christ (this was papist superstition), nor did the body and blood literally accompany the elements, as most Lutherans believed. But nonetheless the Christ was spiritually present. This often seemed a milder doctrine, but in fact, as early Presbyterians interpreted it, it became perhaps the most powerful and moving conception of the divine presence in any Christian tradition. Thus, even in its beginnings the communion service was at the very center of Presbyterian experience, the most important of all the rituals in the church year.

The communion service, whether held annually or more often in each congregation, soon became a functional replacement for confession and penance, as well as the Eucharist, in

4. Leigh Eric Schmidt, *Scottish Communions and American Revivals: Evangelical Ritual, Sacramental Piety, and Popular Festivity from the Reformation Through the Mid-Nineteenth Century* (Ph.D. diss., Princeton University, 1987), 32–42.

former Catholic practice. In Scotland, as in the rest of re-formed Europe, official changes in church policy, in sanc-tioned doctrines and practices, had least apparent effect on the devotional life of lay people. Even after a hundred years some of the old Catholic communion practices lingered in Scot-land, and much more than any Presbyterian would have ad-mitted probably forced Protestant ministers to develop func-tional substitutes. Since Presbyterians had stripped away most of the colorful ceremonies, the festivals and holy days, of Ca-tholicism, lay people craved a substitute, and the expanding communion service alone provided this. Soon after 1600 in Galloway, and after 1613 in Ulster, a few ministers began add-ing more and more preparatory steps to the communion—a day of fasting and prayer, powerful sermons at least on the preceding Friday and Saturday, the careful screening of poten-tial communicants by ministers and the use of small lead to-kens to admit them to the table, and after communion Sunday a follow-up thanksgiving service on Monday. In later lan-guage, they began to turn the communion time into a revival meeting, with a form of preaching and exhortation quite dif-ferent from the weekly pastoral sermon and a level of emo-tional intensity that made these occasions the ones most likely to lead to conversion. In another sense the great communions, which usually involved all the parishes for miles around, be-came a festival or fair, the most exciting time of the year, with thousands of noncommunicants attending. The joint services were a proper time for courtship, for the formation of new friendships, and for various reasons a time of joy and celebra-tion. For the most devout Presbyterians, communion was usually the peak experience of the year; at some communions it could be the peak experience of a lifetime.[5]

In the 1620s, as if in reaction to official efforts to restore a more Anglican communion service in Scotland (including ob-ligatory kneeling), exciting revivals erupted in both south-

5. Ibid., 36–45, 47–49.

west Scotland and in Ulster. Most, if not all, the excitement
accompanied the joint communion services, which became a
defiant expression of Reformed piety. For the first time, the
normal weeping that occurred during the self-examination
and penance that came before communion, and the tears of joy
that came after the reenactment of Christ's passion, yielded to
more intense feeling and more extravagant bodily effects. In
Ulster, the first "wild" services began under an eloquent but
soon deranged minister, peaking in 1624 under the leadership
of a former Glasgow professor, Robert Blair. This series of
revivals, most tied to communion services, became famous in
Ulster Presbyterianism as the Six-Mile-Water Revival, named
after a river and valley. In these protracted communions,
which moved almost weekly from parish to parish, people
came from miles away, found room and board with host families, and often spent all night in agonizing religious services.
The crowds required that most of the preaching be outdoors,
on permanent canopied platforms or what the Presbyterians
called tents, which became common near rural churches. It
was in these Ulster communions that we first have reports of
people fainting dead away and being carried outside in a
trance. When Anglican policies, in part stimulated by concerns over "enthusiasm," forced the Ulster ministers to flee
back to Scotland, up to 500 Ulster Presbyterians crossed the
North Channel to join a former minister in a communion at
Stranraer, in Galloway. Similar revivals had meantime oc-
cured in other areas of Scotland, with the largest and most
remembered communion at Shotts in 1630.[6]

It would not be for decades that communion services again
triggered such exuberant effects, such sweeping revivals of
religion. But the institutional matrix of these revivals, the
extended communion, soon became so habitual and so loved
by the common people that even the most cautious ministers
had to participate and try to keep the festivities as orderly and

6. Ibid., 52–59; Marilyn J. Westerkamp, *Triumph of the Laity: Scots-Irish Piety and the Great
Awakening, 1625–1760* (New York: Oxford University Press, 1988), 23–32.

disciplined as possible. The earlier fervor first revived when Presbyterians were sharply divided during the Commonwealth period. Some communion services in the south of Scotland were so large and so full of religious excitement as to become legendary. Such services marked the second wave of revivals in Scottish Presbyterianism, with widespread reports of massive conversions. A third period of revival began during the Restoration period, when devout rural Presbyterian ministers held illegal clandestine outdoor services and communions, with some attended by thousands of people who not only heard preaching from the tents but sat at huge outdoor tables. Long afterward, James McGready, who led the great sacramental services in Logan County, Kentucky, from 1797 to 1800, referred to these courageous covenanters who risked their lives together for worship in "thickets and deserts." But the largest recorded sacramental services in Scotland paralleled the so-called Great Awakening in the mid-eighteenth century among fellow Presbyterians in America, long after persecution had ended and Presbyterian polity prevailed in Scotland. This revival reached its peak in 1742 at Cambuslang, near Glasgow, in two communions that had an almost erie resemblance to the one at Cane Ridge.[7]

Cambuslang had been an often troubled congregation before 1740, with its lay elders effectively blocking the accession of the minister chosen for them by a local patron. They were finally able to call their choice, William M'Culloch, in 1731. M'Culloch faced difficult early years, with divisions in his Session and profound personal doubts about his own conversion. His early doubts and his repeated periods of intense religious experience made him typical of the most successful evangelical ministers (compare, for instance, John Wesley). He slowly gained confidence, and by 1741 began to rejoice at an awakening in his congregation. This came in the wake of the

7. Schmidt, *Scottish Communions*, 50–54, 66–68, 70–78; James McGready, *The Posthumous Works of the Reverend and Pious James McGready*, ed. James Smith, 2 vols. (Louisville, Ky.: n.p., 1831), 2:134–35.

splintering off of the Associate Synod (the Seceders) and deep rifts in the Scottish church. Perhaps more critical, George Whitefield, home from revival triumphs in America and full of accounts of the awakening there, preached ten sermons in Glasgow in 1741. Many members of the Cambuslang congregation walked the five miles to attend these massive outdoor services. In the winter of 1741–42 the Cambuslang congregation almost exploded with religious fervor. Prayer circles met continually, M'Culloch soon had to preach every day, Sunday services were overcrowded, and almost all local sinners were deeply affected if not converted before the summer. These circumstances provided the setting for the annual communion season, normally the highlight of the church year. It more than lived up to expectations.

The first of the two communions that year (and the only regular one) occurred on July 11. The preparatory fasts and preaching began during the week. People at a great distance knew that something unprecedented might happen. The arrival of Whitefield on Friday, and by special invitation of M'Culloch, increased interest and expectations. In preparation the congregation erected two tents (rather like the construction of band shells today) in a natural amphitheater near the meetinghouse, which seems to have been under repair and unusable. They therefore set the long communion tables among the broom that covered the brae. Thousands came. Many stood in long queues for hours on Saturday in order to persuade M'Culloch to give them tokens. On communion Sunday the throng exceeded any ever recorded in Scotland, with some estimates of 30,000 in attendance. Approximately 1,700 communed in multiple settings that took all day. Whitefield gave a memorable sermon in the evening, after the communion was over. Small groups of people, under deep conviction, talked all the night. Whitefield preached the thanksgiving sermon on Monday, after which people were reluctant to leave. No one could estimate the number converted. Almost every conceivable physical exercise, including falling in a swoon, afflicted some participants. The ministers deplored disruptive behavior during the services, but in spite of their appeals many cried out, even during communion, and in later interviews swore they could not control themselves however much they tried.

In an unprecedented action, the Session decided to hold a second communion that same summer, scheduled for August 15. By then the first communion had become famous, a subject of extended controversy in Scotland. Whitefield returned; he would not have missed this second communion for his life. People came from England, Ireland, and in large numbers from Edinburgh. Possibly the numbers did approach 30,000 at this service. By careful count, 3,000 took communion, in all probability a record for all time in a single Scottish communion. The last table was served at sunset. Some cried because they had been unable to get tokens. The crowd made it almost impossible for some to get to the tables. Twelve ministers served different settings. Whitefield was able to give his exhortation only at ten o'clock Sunday night. On Monday, with many extra ministers free from their own pastoral duties, twenty-four clergymen attended the thanksgiving services. For Whitefield the August communion was a highlight of his career, for "such a Passover has not yet been heard of." Three or four other local communions were almost as large and the awakening spread throughout Scotland, but nothing in the history of evangelical Presbyterianism ever quite equaled these two sacraments at Cambuslang. Their symbolic significance in Scotland rivaled that of the later Cane Ridge communion in America.

In Scotland and Ulster, as later in America, these huge regional communions proved very divisive. The extended communion normally functioned as a routine ritual that was loved by almost all Scottish Presbyterians. The extended services, which convened at set times each year, helped maintain loyalty to the church. One could compare them to decorous retreats organized in modern churches. But in the three or four waves of revival, the huge rural gatherings, with all the extreme physical exercises, dismayed or frightened possibly a majority of Presbyterian clergymen. Support for, or criticism of, wild and seemingly unruly mobs of lay people helped mark a rather clear rupture within Presbyterianism, a rupture related to issues of style and practice, not clearly to doctrine or intellectuality. As in America, the revivalistic style did not always correlate with lower educational attainment (often just the opposite), or with any clear break with the Westminster Confession (again, often just the opposite, for Arminianism and incipient universalism predominated among the more rationalist and formal Presbyterians). Correctly, Cambuslang was the focus of much of the controversy. Within nine years at least fifty-eight books, plus endless articles, either praised or condemned it.[8]

Unique among all the great Scottish communions, those at Cambuslang became the subject of almost immediate investigation. M'Culloch, aware of their significance and anxious to defend their integrity, began the same year to document their effect on lay participants. He worked out a questionnaire and gave pen and paper to thirty-five men and seventy-one women in his congregation in order to record "God's dealings with their souls." These simple folk were not only passably literate but at times voluble. Finally, as a defense against widely circulated charges that such wild and emotional conversions were delusive and thus had no lasting effect, M'Culloch nine years later carried out as extensive a survey as possible among the still-living converts of the great revival of 1742. He located approximately 400 apparently authentic converts from various congregations who had persevered for those nine years, including about 100 who had earlier filled out his questionnaire. This survey had implications for American revivals. The great communion at Cane Ridge

8. This account of Cambuslang is largely drawn from one book, Arthur Fawcett, *The Cambuslang Revival: The Scottish Evangelical Revival of the Eighteenth Century* (London: Banner of Truth Trust, 1971).

in 1801, and other related communions among Presbyterians in America, created so much retrospective interest in Cambuslung that a new evangelical magazine in Pittsburgh published M'Culloch's evaluation, both to inform American readers and as a way of defending what many saw as the excesses of revival.

A brief summary hardly does justice to M'Culloch's questionnaire and subsequent reappraisal. For some communicants, these two great communions were momentous events, almost beyond any verbal description. Some respondents were so honest, or used such vivid sexual imagery, that later editors deleted passages when they published excerpts of the confessions. Some, by their understanding, pushed beyond Presbyterian doctrine, giving ammunition to those who charged the Cambuslang communicants with enthusiasm (claims of direct divine revelation) or ties to the much-hated French Prophets (the Camisards, a radical wing of the French Reformed church whose physical exercises and claims of divine guidance made them extreme antinomians). The effects on the local congregation were lasting, although the revival ebbed very quickly. Conversions continued until 1748, but with annual decreases. Crimes all but ceased in the immediate aftermath, but not for long. Approximately four out of five converts remained in the church for the next decade, although not at the level of zeal that marked 1742. The falloff, noted sadly by M'Culloch, was no worse, and possibly not as sharp, as for people who came into the church in normal times. Before 1742, only 400 or 500 communed each season, and many of these would have been from neighboring congregations. By 1745 the number was down from 3,000 to 1,300 and falling, but it remained much higher than before.[9]

By the mid-eighteenth century, much of the external criti-

---

9. Ibid., 4–8, 163–81; William M'Culloch, "Attestations on the Cambuslang Revival," reprinted in *Western Missionary Magazine* 2 (August 1804): 122–32; (September 1804): 161–68. Schmidt provides a detailed analysis of the gathered testimonials (*Scottish Communions*, 186–212).

cism of the huge communions focused not on the communicants, but on the always much larger horde of spectators. Despite carefully developed rules, no one could control the behavior of those who came, observed, ridiculed, or exploited the occasion. They remained on the fringes of the religious services. Some came for fun, some to socialize, some to market goods, some for assignations with lovers. To them, communion was carnival. Secular critics saw such affairs as a throwback to the medieval past, an embarrassment to Scotland in its age of enlightenment. Rowdy youth openly ridiculed the communion services or held mock ones. Robert Burns wrote a heavily satirical poem, "The Holy Fair," as a way of ridiculing the sacrament and highlighting the alleged hypocrisy of the overly serious and outwardly pious Presbyterian organizers.[10] Thus, a central and distinguishing institution of Presbyterianism was under attack, both from within and without, in the second half of the eighteenth century. At the same time, Ulster emigrants were just establishing the same institution in the New World, where, at least for a while, it was safe from both clerical and secular criticism. Cane Ridge was the next Cambuslang.

10. Schmidt, *Scottish Communions*, 244–58.

CHAPTER ONE

American Origins

The development of American Presbyterianism, and thus the institutional path to Cane Ridge, largely involved Scotch-Irish immigrants. But before their massive eighteenth-century immigration, a few scattered English dissenters and a few Scottish Presbyterians founded an infant Presbyterian movement in the American colonies. Nature prevented an earlier, more dramatic beginning. In 1636 a group of Ulster Presbyterians, under legal obligation to affirm the Thirty-nine Articles of the English church and with their ministers already in exile in Scotland, accepted a written invitation from the Massachusetts Bay Colony to settle in New England. Their ship, the *Eagle Wing,* met such storms off Newfoundland that it had to return to Ireland.[1] But soon after, a few English Presbyterians did move to Connecticut, New York (Long Island), and New Jersey, and by 1700 had formed a few small congregations.

In 1706 seven scattered Presbyterian ministers founded the Philadelphia Presbytery, the first in America. The convening minister, Francis MacKemie, was from Ulster, and had organized Presbyterian congregations on the eastern shore of Maryland by 1690. He also briefly lived and preached across the nearby border in Virginia. United with him were three other Maryland ministers (one from Ireland, two from Scot-

1. Marilyn J. Westerkamp, *Triumph of the Laity: Scots-Irish Piety and the Great Awakening, 1625–1760* (New York: Oxford University Press, 1988), 36.

land), two ministers from Delaware (one from New England, the other from Ireland) and the minister at Philadelphia (a New Englander). The presbytery grew rapidly, particularly as it added churches in Pennsylvania and New Jersey, most of English or Puritan heritage. In 1716 the Philadelphia Presbystery upgraded itself into a synod, with three regional presbyteries.

By 1730, abetted by a growing wave of Scotch-Irish immigration, the church had expanded to include the congregations of approximately thirty ministers. By then, the clear majority of ministers had immigrated from Northern Ireland, some moving with whole congregations. In the years before the American Revolution, possibly as many as 150,000 (probably less, although the number is a point of continuing controversy) Scotch-Irish came to America, with the first large wave after 1717, the last just before the Revolution. Early immigrants preferred to settle in New England because of religious affinities and a failure to anticipate Puritan intolerance, but later a majority of new immigrants shifted to Pennsylvania, which offered complete religious liberty and excellent land. For a brief period after 1731 South Carolina offered incentives and religious tolerance, leading to a brief flurry of Irish landings at Charleston, but the Anglican church posed barriers in the rest of the South. From Pennsylvania the Scotch-Irish moved mainly south and west, and soon made up at least half the population in the Piedmont and subsequently over half the early pioneers across the Appalachians.[2]

Only a minority of Scotch-Irish immigrants were able at first to form churches. Over half paid their way to America by indenture. Possibly a majority had not been faithful church members even back in Ulster. Some may have rejoiced in escaping church discipline. But, as in the first emigration from Scotland to Ulster after 1607, many felt a sense of deprivation, or perhaps guilt. Clusters of Scotch-Irish settlers continually

2. R. J. Dickson, *Ulster Emigration to Colonial America, 1718–1775* (London: Routledge and Kegan Paul, 1966), 19–81; James G. Leyburn, *The Scotch-Irish: A Social History* (Chapel Hill: University of North Carolina Press, 1962), 157–83.

petitioned synods in Ulster or even in Scotland to send ministers to America. They never had enough, and ministerial
shortages would place an enduring limit on Presbyterian
growth. By 1741, out of fifty-four Presbyterian ministers in
America, fully twenty-nine had immigrated from Ireland but
only three from Scotland. The others were native-born Americans, many from New England. After this, an increasing proportion of ministers, as one might expect, would be native-
born, but a majority of these had Irish roots.

Early on, tensions developed between Presbyterians of English origin, as in New England, and those directly from Ulster. The immigrants desired the tight discipline of their home
churches and gladly vested centralized power in presbyteries
and synods. Actual conflict developed over subscription to
the Westminster Confession (an issue that also split the church
in Ireland, with the nonsubscribers eventually becoming a liberal, even unitarian splinter group). A majority (but not all) of
the Irish-born ministers desired such uniformity, while most
New Englanders opposed.

None of these ethnic differences fractured the Presbyterian
synod, although synod records reveal continued conflict and
also continual difficulties in settling lay charges against ministers. Generally, American Presbyterians were loyal to the
Westminster Confession, and thus to a rigorous Calvinism,
whether ministers wanted to subscribe or not. In other words,
the American church remained orthodox in a century in
which rationalist and latitudinarian views grew apace. Inroads
of rationalism had much greater influence in Ireland and Scotland than in America, reflecting a perhaps understandable con-
ventionalism among immigrants. In the case of a clearly Arminian, almost deist minister, Samuel Hemphill, who came
over to the Philadelphia church, the synod tried and expelled
him without dissent, gaining thereby the undying contempt
of Benjamin Franklin, who loved Hemphill's eloquent but
largely plagiarized sermons. The actual splitting of the synod
came later, not on points of Calvinist doctrine or over modes

of subscription or adoption but over the fervor that accompanied what many would call the Great Awakening.[3]

It is very difficult to define, locate, or date "revivals" among early American Presbyterians. The Scotch-Irish celebrated their three- or four-day communions as soon as they were able to establish churches and gain ministers. Insofar as geography permitted, these were intercongregational affairs, with multiple ministers presiding. The evidence is slight, but in almost every year one or another minister was able to report stirring services, with conversions and new members. It is even possible that, in some of these communions, the level of emotional intensity and the physical response paralleled those of the great Scottish and Irish revivals of a century earlier. The first widely reported stirring of religion in New Jersey in the late 1720s coincided with the first wave of Scotch-Irish immigration, and from then on paralleled the almost explosive growth of Presbyterianism.

The first leaders of a distinctive revival faction were William Tennent and his four sons. From Ireland, but formerly an Anglican minister who married the daughter of an Ulster Presbyterian, Tennent upon immigration to America successfully applied for fellowship in the Presbyterian synod, which best fitted his low church, evangelical preferences. In 1726 he established himself permanently at Neshaminy in Bucks County, Pennsylvania, where in 1735 he opened a famous academy and informal seminary for aspiring ministers. Called the Log College, it served a vital role in Presbyterianism since the growing church could not continue to import all its ministers from Ulster, while few native candidates could afford to attend Harvard or Yale. Soon a dozen or so of Tennent's students made up an especially fervent circle in the church, for they embraced

3. Leyburn, *The Scotch-Irish*, 145–64; Leigh Eric Schmidt, *Scottish Communions and American Revivals: Evangelical Ritual, Sacramental Piety, and Popular Festivity from the Reformation Through the Mid-Nineteenth Century* (Ph.D. diss., Princeton University, 1987), 88–96; "Minutes of the Synod of Philadelphia," in *Records of the Presbyterian Church in the United States of America, 1706–1788* (New York: Arno, 1969), 9–154.

a warm, experiential approach to religion. Gilbert Tennent, the eldest and most gifted son, took a master of arts degree at Yale in 1725 and then ministered to a congregation in New Brunswick, New Jersey. His ability in the pulpit (he was known as the "Son of Thunder") and his fervor made him a leader of the most revivalist faction in Presbyterianism, while his perennial tours throughout the colonies made him the most influential itinerant evangelist in America save for the English (and Anglican) orator, George Whitefield.[4]

The label "Great Awakening" is confusing. It suggests one vast, related, colony-wide revival of religion. The actual phenomenon was much more complex. Almost from the time of colonization, certain ministers among New England Puritans and, later, among middle colony Dutch Reformed or Presbyterian congregations reported exciting interludes when sermons were well attended, when individuals came under deep conviction, and when numerous persons gave convincing testimony to conversion and thus were admitted to the communion table. Most such periods of awakening remained quite local, keyed often to the effectiveness of a single minister. The timing varied from place to place, and the linkages were few. But such revivals were usually contagious enough to spread to at least a few nearby congregations. This happened in New Jersey in the 1720s, in the Connecticut Valley after Jonathan Edwards's success in 1734 at Northampton, and, primarily because of the role of George Whitefield, at several points in New England and the middle colonies from 1739 to 1742. By then published accounts, such as Edwards's *A Faithful Narrative of the Surprising Work of God,* and the intercolonial ties created by Whitefield and others ensured widespread publicity even for local revivals. An increasing number of ministers, such as Gilbert Tennent, learned from Whitefield and took to the road, traveling widely on behalf of revivals that finally were much more than regional, even more than national

4. Westerkamp, *Triumph of the Laity,* 167–68.

events, since the new networks crossed the Atlantic and correlated with widespread revivals in England, Scotland, and
Northern Ireland. The commonalities, the interactions, and
the scope of such revivals, particularly in the 1740s, gave
some content to the title of a great awakening, if not *the*
Great Awakening.

Of all Protestant churches in America, the Scotch-Irish
Presbyterians enjoyed the most suitable institutional setting
for periodic revivals. The great communions provided the
single most significant continuity between the eighteenth-
century awakenings and both nineteenth-century camp meetings and protracted revivals within congregations. Not that
the communions provided the only precedent. Association
meetings and intercongregational baptisms among Baptists,
quarterly and annual conferences among Methodists, presbyterial and synodical meetings among Presbyterians—all
helped shape such nineteenth-century institutions. But nothing was as conducive to cyclical revivals as the traditional
communion service, with its day of fasting and prayer, its in-
tensive all-day preparatory services, the careful screening of
candidates and allocation of tokens (which very conspicu-
ously identified those outside the church), the intense experience of the sacrament itself, and the follow-up thanksgiving service, all in an intercongregational context with huge
throngs of people, outdoor preaching tents, and frequent all-
night prayer services. Add to this the special fellowship created by the visiting members of other congregations, even the
large number of curious observers or spectators who came
and, often without intent, were pulled into the intensely emotional sacramental service.

Thus, in all the mid-eighteenth-century revivals, the primary institutional setting among Presbyterians remained the
great Scottish communion. This would remain true for the
even more extensive Presbyterian revivals that occurred from
Pennsylvania to western Kentucky between 1797 and 1805, or
what some would call the Second Great Awakening. But the

image of only two explosions is misleading. Among Presbyterians, at least, unusually inspiring and dramatic Sunday services or communions occurred somewhere almost every year from 1740 to 1797. Some of the early communions clearly presaged the one at Cane Ridge and produced memories and expectations that help explain what happened there.

Through the 1730s and 1740s, the more experientially oriented Presbyterian ministers reported ever better attended and glorious sacramental seasons, as well as wonderful "sabbath" services. Gilbert Tennent and other ministers reported thousands in attendance at some joint communions, where almost all the preaching necessarily took place outdoors from the traditional tent. So did most of the preaching by Whitefield when he toured the middle colonies in 1739. And the more effective preaching, such as that by Whitefield, elicited an unprecedented display of feeling—weeping, groaning, and crying out for mercy. Whitefield's description of one Presbyterian congregation included a portrayal of people as "pale as death," and others lying on the ground in the trancelike state first noted in the Ulster revival of 1624. Because of widespread charges of enthusiasm or antinomianism and of a growing opposition to wild services and lay excesses, Presbyterian ministers often talked only generally about "physical exercises," or even tried to conceal or minimize the most extravagant lay behavior. Yet even by the 1740s almost all the exercises that Cane Ridge would make famous, including not only sobbing, shouting, and swooning but also bodily convulsions or jerks, had erupted in one or more congregations.[5]

As in Scotland, the more extreme exercises worried almost all Presbyterian ministers and elicited condemnation from at least a minority. This Presbyterian caution did little to abate the exercises and proved costly in time. Out of the revivals of the 1740s came several Separate Baptist congregations, a movement that spread from New England to the South by the

5. Schmidt, *Scottish Communions*, 93–104.

1750s. These Baptists, although Calvinist in doctrine, seemed to have few qualms about highly emotional services or extreme bodily effects, a difference in style that separated them from the more staid Particular Baptists who had preceded them in the middle and southern colonies. Thus, what Presbyterians tried to understand and control, these Baptists made normative. In time they gained the most converts.[6]

In the midst of the most fervent revivals, the Synod of Philadelphia split (in sentiment by 1741, institutionally in 1745) over several divisive issues, not the least being the status of the more extreme physical exercises. Gilbert Tennent and his brothers first helped establish a very evangelistic presbytery, that of New Brunswick. Most of its ministers had ties to William Tennent's Log College. Their group behavior soon alienated a majority of their ministerial colleagues. New Brunswick licensed ministers who lacked the normal educational requirements but confessed a plenitude of experiential piety. The Philadelphia Synod responded with such tough educational requirements for ministers as to challenge the Log College tradition. The New Brunswick Presbytery asserted its autonomy in licensing ministers as against the synod. Meanwhile, often in response to lay requests, Log College men became itinerants and preached in local congregations against the wishes of the local, or at least neighboring, clergy, sometimes deeply dividing congregations.

The climax of the developing split came in 1740. In a thinly veiled challenge to many older, established ministers, Gilbert Tennent preached his famous, widely published sermon, "The Danger of an Unconverted Ministry." Although its vehement and overt attack on "cold and sapless" sermons that froze on the lips of ministers "not sent of God" best described Anglicans and deists, many of his colleagues who lacked Tennent's fervor or pulpit style felt it was aimed at them. The ministers who thought themselves thus vilified, including

6. Wesley M. Gewehr, *The Great Awakening in Virginia, 1740–1790* (Durham: Duke University Press, 1930), 106–37.

about half the Scotch-Irish immigrant ministers, were incensed. They felt beleaguered as they tried to maintain professional standards of collegiality, traditional educational requirements for ministers, a centralized church order, and careful adherence to the Westminster Confession. Perhaps above all, they feared the new, more florid, less systematic style of preaching, and although not opposed to all aspects of the revivals, they lamented the effects of the new preaching on weaker lay people, who often cried out or fell down in convulsion-like fits.[7]

Both sides (the Old Side Philadelphia Synod and the New Side New York Synod) remained nominally orthodox in doctrine, and soon after the split both began softening their positions. Reunion occurred in 1758, largely on New Side terms. The Old Side had a declining appeal to lay people, who seem never to have become much involved in what was largely a ministerial struggle, but whose taste in preaching clearly favored Tennent and his colleagues. While the schism lasted, the lines of development from one awakening to another, and thus the road to Cane Ridge, lay in the rapid spread of Presbyterianism to Virginia and the Carolinas. In most cases the missionary work was by the New Side, but not always. By the time southern Presbyterianism was well established, the schism was over.

In a strict sense, Presbyterianism began in the South, since some of the first congregations were in Maryland. But early Presbyterian growth was to the north, centering on Pennsylvania and New Jersey as the Scotch-Irish flocked to the middle colonies. Soon, however, they found better economic prospects farther west. The largest number disembarked at Philadelphia, flooded the German areas west toward the mountains, and by 1730 began moving through the Alleghenies.

---

7. Westerkamp, *Triumph of the Laity*, 167–94; Gilbert Tennent, "The Dangers of an Unconverted Ministry," in *The Great Awakening: Documents on the Revival of Religion, 1740–1745*, ed. Richard L. Bushman (New York: Atheneum, 1970), 87–93. The institutional history of the split is in "Minutes of the Synod of Philadelphia," 143–84.

From central Pennsylvania they moved along with German sects into the Shenandoah Valley of Virginia by the mid-1730s. By 1736 Presbyterian settlers in Augusta County had formed two congregations and successfully requested visits by ministers from eastern presbyteries. In 1740 a congregation near Staunton called a permanent minister, John Craig, just over from Ireland (and thus sympathetic to the Old Side) as the first settled Presbyterian minister in Virginia. Fortunately, far from Williamsburg, these congregations suffered no opposition from civil authorities. Soon Presbyterian congregations dotted the valley from Winchester to Lexington. Eventually these valley churches provided at least half the Presbyterian settlers of the Holston Valley in what is now southwest Virginia and east Tennessee, of the central counties in what is now Kentucky, and of the Cumberland area in middle Tennessee and south Kentucky, or the points of origin for the great revival symbolized by Cane Ridge.[8]

The second flowering of Virginia Presbyterianism, and one even more directly related to the western revivals, occurred not in the Shenandoah Valley but in the more populous Virginia Piedmont, around the developing city of Richmond. There the dominant early figure was Samuel Davies, a very young, brilliant, politically astute Presbyterian minister, whose role in southern Presbyterianism almost rivaled that of his admired friend Jonathan Edwards among Congregationalists in the Connecticut Valley. Davies joined colleagues in a belated effort to lure the great Edwards to Virginia in 1751, and would succeed him in the presidency of the College of New Jersey at Princeton in 1758, even imitating Edwards by his premature death in 1761 in that by then cursed presidency.

Davies, of Welsh rather than Irish lineage, was born in Delaware in 1723. As a young man already inclined to the ministry, Davies enrolled in another famous Presbyterian academy at Faggs Manor, south of Philadelphia, the spiritual offspring of

8. William Henry Foote, *Sketches of Virginia, Historical and Biographical*, vol. 1 (Philadelphia: Martien, 1850), 98–106; vol. 2 (Philadelphia: Lippincott, 1855), 13–40.

William Tennent's Log College. The master was Samuel Blair, a Log College man and almost as successful a revivalist as Gilbert Tennent. Although his health was fragile, Davies was a dedicated student, gaining ordination in 1747, after which he was assigned by his presbytery as an evangelist to new congregations in Hanover County, Virginia.

The Hanover congregations, which shortly formed the Hanover Presbytery, at first made up an anomalous, non-ethnic branch of American Presbyterianism. In Hanover County a small number of lay people, influenced by the revivals of 1741 and the preaching of Whitefield, had formed dissenting discussion groups. They read Luther and other reformed writers, and soon thirsted for a more experiential piety than they found in their Anglican churches. They first met in homes, which they called reading houses, and then built houses of worship, resulting in the arrest of their leaders for holding unlicensed religious services. Soon such evangelical Anglicans would find their own niche in Methodist societies, but at this early date they knew nothing about the Wesleyan movement just beginning in England. When the evangelicals were hauled before the colonial council, a sympathetic Governor William Gooch, who as a Scotsman was familiar with Presbyterianism, so labeled the beliefs of the local dissenters, who were as yet unfamiliar with the Scottish church. As nominal Presbyterians, they came under the Act of Toleration. Subsequently, these uninstructed "Presbyterians" asked for support, and ministers, from the New Brunswick Presbytery. One of the first visiting Presbyterian ministers, the fiery William Robinson, used offerings from these congregations to help fund young Davies's education at Blair Academy, thus creating a debt which Davies subsequently repaid.

Except for a series of visiting ministers, and a telling visit by Whitefield, all unlicensed to preach in Virginia and thus subject to arrest, the Hanover congregations were leaderless until Davies arrived in 1747. Although an inexperienced youth, he went first to Williamsburg and secured from an impressed governor and council a license to preach among the Presbyterians. In the next decade he carried on a ceaseless, difficult, but usually successful struggle to gain toleration for a growing number of Presbyterian congregations in central Virginia, most originally organized by himself. The Anglican gentry of Virginia, of higher social status than Davies but of decidedly inferior intellectual abilities, feared and resented the dissenting congregations, and never with good grace accepted the applicability of the Act of Toleration to Virginia. To win even begrudging toleration, Davies had to address several carefully written appeals to various authorities in England.[9]

Davies brought to central Virginia the New Side emphasis on religious affections but also demanded a rigorous intellectuality. He closely followed Jonathan Edwards, arguing that his literate, often prospering Virginia parishioners would not tolerate a religion based only on sentiment or feeling. From 1747 to 1755, Davies was able to organize about a dozen congregations around Richmond and to introduce his original English flock to the old religion of Scotland, including its extended communion services. He helped attract a half-dozen like-minded young ministers, who joined in a period of almost continuous revival and growth. In 1755 these congregations separated into a new Hanover Presbytery. By then most new members reflected the heavy Scotch-Irish immigration, not further conversion of Anglicans (who soon turned to the preferred alternative offered by Methodist societies).

Davies and his associated ministers deserve special mention in American religious history because of their success in converting blacks. Davies made this ministry one of his highest priorities, and successfully solicited financial support, and plenty of praise, from the London Society for Promoting Religious Knowledge Among the Poor. Sporadic earlier efforts to evangelize African slaves had led to meager results, although

9. Schmidt, *Scottish Communions*, 99–101; Foote, *Sketches of Virginia* 1:119–41, 157–221; Rhys Isaacs, *The Transformation of Virginia, 1740–1790* (Chapel Hill: University of North Carolina Press, 1982), 148–57.

at times to baptisms. The New Side religion proved very appealing to blacks, and the young ministers went out of their way to convert them. One early associate of Davies's, John Todd, had in his congregation over fifty slaves, most from the plantation of William Byrd II, and at one extended communion accepted forty-four slaves to the tables. This is an astonishing number, because the ministers would not give out communion tokens until converts understood the Shorter Catechism, which made literacy crucial. Another minister, John Wright, taught two Sunday schools (literacy schools) for blacks each Sunday, both before and after the worship service. Davies invited slaves to come to his home on Saturday evenings for instruction, the only period they were free from work. He was appalled at the failure of Anglicans to instruct their "poor neglected Negroes," and reported at one time that up to 300 blacks attended services in his ministry (that is, in the seven congregations he organized and served). He baptized about 100. They sat, undoubtedly segregated, in the churches, attentive, he said, to every word. In some southern Virginia congregations blacks made up approximately half the membership.

Davies found many slaves serious and sincere, even if simple in their understanding of the gospel. At his house, many blacks lingered after Saturday instruction, some spending the night in Davies's kitchen. He found that blacks, "above all the human species I ever knew," had an ear for music, and thus he secured from England copies of Isaac Watts's hymns to distribute among them. The need to read the hymnbooks became a powerful motive toward literacy. Once Davies awoke at three in the morning to hear the blacks in his kitchen still singing hymns—"a torrent of sacred harmony poured into my chamber, and carried my mind away to heaven." Most masters, even when unchurched, cooperated to the extent of permitting their slaves to attend Presbyterian services.[10]

10. Samuel Davies to Society in London for Promoting Religious Knowledge Among the Poor, March 1755, in Foote, *Sketches of Virginia* 1:284–87. See also other correspondence of Davies and his colleagues as recorded in ibid., 287–93.

These few windows on the story of early black Presbyterians in the Virginia Piedmont cannot support sweeping conclusions. Somehow within the next century, most slaves became Christians, although they apparently blended some aspects of their earlier African religions with Christianity. Davies's observation in Virginia was that, in 1750, almost none were Christian, that masters so far had sadly ignored their spiritual welfare, and that blacks (half the local population by his estimate) were essentially without any religion. Davies noted no African survivals. In his perspective, he and his colleagues began the evangelization of southern blacks. He was undoubtedly wrong in seeing all of the influence flowing in one direction. In ways impossible to decipher from the evidence, blacks must have had some effect on southern Presbyterianism—at the very least on hymn singing and possibly on the range of physical exercises accepted at times of revival.

This unprecedented openness to blacks remained a distinguishing mark of Presbyterianism as it expanded through southern Virginia into the Carolinas. But in the long term, the Presbyterians were not in the best position to recruit blacks. They won the earliest converts because they offered to blacks the first available form of a warm, evangelical Christianity. But the path to full communion was still arduous. It is clear that Davies and his associates accepted some illiterate blacks to communion, but only reluctantly and on the basis of at least their oral comprehension of the catechism. In other words, they tried to nurture blacks toward membership in much the same way they did their own youth. Subsequently, both Methodists and Baptists offered blacks the same warm religion, even the same appealing hymns, all without such rigorous intellectual demands. Eventually, most of the blacks from the Byrd plantation converted to Baptism. As so often in the South, Presbyterians prepared the way but then lost out in the subsequent competition. But at least from 1750 on southern Presbyterianism was biracial. In fact, blacks almost always composed the largest non-Irish component of southern Presbyterian congregations.

Davies served his church for only a decade. Even so, he spent one of these years in Britain, establishing contacts with evangelicals there and raising funds for the new College of New Jersey. By his death at Princeton in 1761, the first wave of revivals and the period of rapid growth of Presbyterianism in central Virginia were over. By then the Baptists were the most effective proselytizers, while the existing Presbyterian congregations in the Richmond area, soon attended by a social elite, prospered materially but enjoyed limited growth. The area of expansion shifted to southern Virginia and the Carolinas. As early as 1738, colonies of Scotch-Irish moved to southern Virginia, particularly to Prince Edward and Charlotte counties. Soon after Davies came to Hanover County, he and his early colleagues preached periodically in these new congregations, which were part of the Hanover Presbytery and soon attracted permanent ministers. These Presbyterians eventually matured a local academy into the first struggling southern Presbyterian college, Hampden-Sydney. Revivals at this college after the Revolution would lead directly to that at Cane Ridge.[11]

By 1750, several Presbyterian families had moved into the Piedmont of North Carolina, some up from South Carolina, most down from Pennsylvania. Many had close connections with southern Virginia congregations. Traveling ministers, such as the fervent New Side and Log College missionary William Robinson, preached to scattered groups of Presbyterians in North Carolina in the years before 1747. As early as 1744 the Synod of Philadelphia received urgent requests from North Carolina for ministers. It sent only visiting evangelists. In 1755 an Irish-born licentiate, Hugh McAden, first began an extended missionary effort in the Carolinas in areas that would soon also attract several Baptist congregations. In 1757, upon ordination, McAden moved to congregations in eastern North Carolina as the first settled Presbyterian minister in the Carolinas, in an area well east of the later growth

11. Foote, *Sketches of Virginia* 1:393–408.

of the church. Subsequently, in part for health reasons, he moved to Caswell County, close to the congregations of southern Virginia.

After 1760 five other ministers joined McAden, all in the Piedmont area. In 1770 these ministers formed a new presbytery, that of Orange. The founding generation of Carolina ministers recruited or trained most of the Presbyterian preachers who presided over the great western revivals at the turn of the coming century. The ministerial fellowship among southern Presbyterians remained almost familial in the prerevolutionary South. With few exceptions, all were Scotch-Irish. Most had earlier roots in the middle colonies, particularly Pennsylvania. They had all attended a few Presbyterian academies. They met in presbytery and synod and shared in summer communions. Many enjoyed kinship ties through intermarriage. The members of their congregations varied in wealth and education, but in the Piedmont generally reflected a landed, literate, politically involved class of people. (Until Baptists and Methodists had made successful inroads on its congregations, southern Presbyterianism remained a class-inclusive, ethnic denomination.) In other words, early Presbyterians, even when most still lived in rude log houses, were the leading citizens of their backcountry counties. From them would later come a disproportionate share of governors, professional people, and educators. In fact, in higher education Presbyterians dominated both private and public universities in North Carolina for the next century. Even before the Revolution they were a social notch above the competing Baptists, and much above the few early Methodists. Only North Carolina Anglicans could claim a higher social status than Presbyterians, but they rarely had active congregations in the most heavily Presbyterian counties.[12]

By 1760 Scotch-Irish Presbyterians faced stiff competition in recruiting new members and even in retaining their own

12. William Henry Foote, *Sketches of North Carolina, Historical and Biographical* (New York: Carter, 1846), 158–99, 213–43.

youth. Particularly in Virginia and North Carolina, they had to accommodate a new form of religious pluralism. Up through the revivals of the 1740s, Presbyterians cooperated and did not really compete with other like-minded Reformed churches, including New England Congregationalists and middle colony Dutch and German Reformed congregations. Cooperation also extended to low church Anglicans. Presbyterians often coexisted with German Lutheran, Moravian, and Anabaptist sects (Mennonites, Amish, Brethren), but language or doctrine kept these bodies fully distinct, with no threats in either direction. Thus, when Scotch-Irish Presbyterians moved south they at first faced no effective religious competition. They merely filled the evangelical niche left open by Anglicans.

This situation changed, at first with the rapid growth of the Separate Baptist movement and then with the prerevolutionary beginnings of Methodism. Overtly Calvinist in doctrine, the Baptists utilized untrained clergymen and featured a fervent style that contrasted sharply with the intellectuality of Presbyterians. The Baptists, who emphasized adult baptism by immersion and held closed communion services, competed for converts openly and flagrantly and refused most forms of cooperation. For their part the Methodists, an American wing of the Wesleyan movement within Anglicanism, began forming societies and ministerial circuits in the South just before the Revolution, enjoyed a blazing revival in Virginia, and soon preempted Presbyterianism in the appeal for converts in almost all Anglican areas of the South. Doctrinally Arminian (unlike staunchly predestinarian Presbyterians), they were nonetheless more open to cooperation than the Baptists, and in a sense were more dangerous competitors for this reason. But the Presbyterians at least had a head start over the Methodists in North Carolina and until the Revolution competed equally with Baptists.[13]

13. Gewehr, 106–66; Isaacs, *Transformation of Virginia*, 161–77, 192–94.

The most influential of early Presbyterian ministers in North Carolina, David Caldwell, became in a sense the grand-father of the great revival. His career also demonstrates the complex interrelationships among the intensely ambitious professional Presbyterian clergy. Born in 1725 of Irish parents in what would soon become Lancaster County, Pennsylvania, he grew up without a classical education on his father's farm. After becoming a carpenter, he experienced a religious conver-sion and decided at age twenty-five to become a Presbyterian minister. He attended a local Presbyterian academy at Pecua, which was presided over by the father of two later presidents of Hampden-Sydney College. Around 1758 he matriculated at the College of New Jersey and completed his baccalaureate in 1761 during the last year of the life of President Samuel Davies.

After graduation Caldwell briefly taught school in New Jer-sey, even as he began the arduous and extended process of obtaining a license and then ordination as a Presbyterian min-ister. After a series of examinations, trial sermons, and mis-sionary tours, he gained ordination in 1765. By then he had probably already decided to move to North Carolina. Several childhood associates in Lancaster County established a Scotch-Irish colony on Buffalo Creek (near the present Greensboro) in what shortly after became Guilford County. Even his ministerial training may have reflected his desire, or the desire of his friends, that he become their minister. Proba-bly in 1764, at age thirty-nine (older than Davies at his death), he visited his people in North Carolina and upon ordination accepted a transfer to the Hanover Presbytery. Although as-signed to North Carolina in 1765, he spent a year in itinerant work among the several still mostly unstaffed congregations throughout the Piedmont. He also bought a farm and spent time developing it. One of his brothers likewise moved to the area along Buffalo Creek to purchase an adjoining farm. To complete these familial connections, Caldwell shortly mar-ried the daughter of an earlier pioneer minister, Alexander

Craighead, who had formerly been a neighbor in Lancaster County. Craighead, always controversial, managed to get himself suspended from his presbytery in Pennsylvania, briefly helped form the first Reformed Presbyterian churches (the old Scotch Covenanter church) in America, then returned to his old church. He served a congregation in the valley until Braddock's defeat in 1755, then fled to Mecklenburg County (the present Charlotte area), where he remained until his death, one of the first three Presbyterian ministers in all North Carolina.

David Caldwell, at age forty, began a sixty-year career (he lived to almost his hundredth birthday) at the Alamanse and Buffalo congregations just outside modern Greensboro. His age and maturity, his Princeton degree, plus a later honorary doctorate all established his high academic credentials. He soon followed the lead of two earlier Presbyterians in other parts of the state and established a classical academy. Despite the requirement of presbyteries that congregations calling a minister subscribe a stated salary, almost no ministers in the eighteenth century could live on their salaries, even when they were successful in collecting them. They thus combined the ministry with either farming or teaching, or both. In time Caldwell's academy gained as much fame as William Tennent's Log College. Caldwell boarded fifty or sixty boys of various ages each year, instructed them in the classical languages, and in the absence of nearby colleges continued some to the college or seminary level. By the Revolution his own log college was incomparably the premier academy in the Piedmont. In it he taught an estimated fifty Presbyterian ministers, most of whom had no other college training. He also taught five later governors and a wide array of judges, lawyers, and physicians. Among his more illustrious family descendants was a grandson, John Caldwell Calhoun. In addition to farming, teaching, and preaching, Caldwell practiced medicine. He was a correspondent with, visitor to, and in a sense a disciple of Dr. Benjamin Rush.

Like Davies, Caldwell played a major public role. He tried, unsuccessfully, to mediate between populistic Piedmont insurgents, called Regulators, and Governor William Tyron in order to resolve a long-brewing backcountry revolt, which ended in 1771 in a pitched battle at Alamanse, near his two churches. He was an active partisan in the American Revolution. General Cornwallis, in his march through North Carolina in 1780, devastated Caldwell's farm and burned his library and personal papers. His brother died in the patriot cause. Caldwell was a delegate to the North Carolina Constitutional Convention, and later a delegate to the convention in 1788 that rejected the new federal constitution. By then he was the best-known Presbyterian in the South. Meanwhile, he regularly attended presbytery, wrote his weekly sermons, and traveled faithfully each summer to neighboring congregations to participate in extended communion services. But what makes his career so critical to the later events at Cane Ridge is that almost all the early revival ministers in the West had some connection to Caldwell. They were literally his boys.[14]

The American Revolution meant hard times in the Piedmont. Presbyterians were divided in their loyalties. Armies on both sides wreaked havoc on the countryside in 1780. Schools and churches were disrupted. Yet a few local ministers continued to report interludes of revival, and several young ministers had joined the presbytery by war's end. In later memory, the immediate postwar years marked a dead time for religion. They were also a period of exodus. After the war, large numbers of Carolina Scotch-Irish began to move over the mountains, seeking better economic opportunities. Caldwell's sister-in-law and nephews moved to Greene County just before Tennessee achieved statehood, and there joined distant relatives from Pennsylvania and neighbors who had moved to the same area from the great Shenandoah Valley of

14. Eli W. Caruthers, *A Sketch of the Life and Character of the Rev. David Caldwell, D.D.* (Greensboro, N.C.: Swaim and Sherwood, 1842), 7–43; Foote, *Sketches of North Carolina*, 231–43.

Virginia. Hezekiah Balch, Caldwell's colleague and one of the original ministers in Orange Presbytery, moved to the same east Tennessee area as a pioneer minister in Greeneville. From the valley churches came Samuel Doak, a minister and educator who built the first Presbyterian academies (later colleges) west of the Blue Ridge Mountains. Doak, like Caldwell, had matriculated at Princeton, and for two war years served as a tutor at Hampden-Sydney. Thomas Craighead, son of Alexander and brother-in-law of David Caldwell, moved even farther, to the distant Cumberland settlements, as the first Presbyterian pastor in the Nashville area. By the last decade of the century, these western Presbyterians addressed numerous pleas and petitions back to their old presbyteries, begging a larger supply of desperately needed ministers. Among the young ministers who answered these calls were those who began the great revival at the turn of the century.

Before any of the young North Carolina ministers moved west, they participated in a new wave of local revivals. This statement begs a dozen questions, beginning with the definition of *revival*. In almost any year, among Baptists, Methodists, or Presbyterians, some local ministers could boast of an exciting period of renewal—more piety, more fervor, numerous conversions, and vastly improved morals. Individual congregations experienced their own cycles, with peaks and valleys in both membership and fervor. Some of these cycles correlated with generational changes, some with ministerial leadership, some with major population shifts, some with local economic or social conditions. Imitation was often crucial as waves of such renewal swept counties or regions. Excitement in one congregation created an almost immediate expectancy, or demand, in neighboring ones. But none of these factors were clearly necessary for revivals, and no set of such factors was clearly sufficient. Causes are hard to come by, and patterns do not fit all cases.

The most conspicuous pattern, one supported by objective data (church membership lists, attendance figures, reports on the moral tenor of a community) as well as by the perceptions of ministers, is that periods of revival almost always followed, and in intensity were in inverse relationship to, years of declension, coldness, impiety, or even apostasy. Consistent with this is another pattern—a revival had a half-life of only two or three years. In five or six years it had always burned out, although its effects did not disappear and a congregation did not necessarily return to its former state. But nonetheless, the phenomenon was self-limiting. In the wake of a great revival, therefore, a given congregation was for a number of years simply not open to a comparable awakening. Metaphors help express this fact. The fuel was missing. Almost everyone, including all the youth, became actively involved in a church. Such a harvest temporarily precluded the deep doubts, the widespread sense of guilt, the unease of conscience that often made up one of the most vital combustibles of a new revival.

At war's end, most Presbyterian ministers in Virginia and North Carolina reported a period of deadness. They blamed it, correctly or not, either on the disruptions of the late war or on the appeal of religious rationalism or deism. As so often, the concern focused on the youth, primarily teenagers but also young adults, or those who had no memory of the stirring revivals of twenty and thirty years earlier. Ministerial laments, or specially organized prayer meetings in hopes of a new revival, reflected parental concerns about "our young people" and reveal the primary generational factor in cyclical revivals.

Busy Presbyterian ministers were as conscientious as time and distance permitted in providing catechism classes for youth. But such instruction did not ensure the confession of experiential piety required for communion, or lead youth to exhibit the type of moral behavior that would make them eligible to come to the table. In the words of the ministers, the young people often did not experience any intense sense of their own depravity or unworthiness, did not go through the drama of remorse and personal repentance, did not know the

sense of comfort or liberation that stood as evidence of a rebirth experience, and consequently did not reflect in their lives
an absorbing love of God or the behavior that should accompany such a love. Indifference and immorality testified to their
lack of faith. Year by year, the number of unconverted youth
could accumulate, creating an intense yearning for revival on
the part of older communicants, and also providing the fuel
for a major revival should something provide the eagerly desired spark.

In most Presbyterian communities, the largest body of potential communicants, sometimes up to half the people normally in a congregation, were such unconverted youth, joined
by a handful of overtly sinful adults. But almost always in
direct proportion to a growing pool of unconverted youth
was a high level of coldness or dullness (their words) among
most church members, and what the more evangelical ministers saw as a lack of zeal, of spirituality, and of appropriate
conduct. This last usually did not mean any gross immorality.
Good, well-reared Presbyterian adults even felt guilty when
they gave in to temptation and attended dances. The problems
were gossip, jealousies, local quarrels, and too much absorption in worldly diversions, including work or business. Given
such trends away from a vital Pauline Christianity, one can ask
why revivals always, as if inevitably, ensued. Why not a pattern of continued decline? The psychological answer lies in the
people who experienced such declension. They remained
fully within the older belief system. They accepted both Semitic theism and the Pauline scheme of salvation. They had
grown up with this worldview, absorbed it from weekly sermons and catechism, and internalized the hopes and dreams
that went with it.

Undoubtedly a few people—and until 1800 they were few
indeed in well-formed Presbyterian congregations—came to
doubt the core beliefs. They could not find in their own experience any validation of the Pauline drama of salvation, and thus
either left the church permanently or helped transform their

congregations into more humanistic and rationalistic alternatives. Such individuals, if they truly attained emancipation
from the old beliefs, rather than flirting briefly with rational
alternatives, were not open either to deep penitence or true
conversion. They might still come to the great communion
services, even take communion, but they did not fully participate in the meaning of the sacrament. But for most people
within the Presbyterian culture, the effect of religious decline,
of worldly diversion, was either deep guilt or the ever-present
potential that, prodded by sermons or neighborly exhortation, they would plunge into intense self-examination.

Given the intensely introspective nature of its salvation doctrines, the cyclical patterns that characterized Scottish Presbyterianism make perfect sense. Instead of a continuous inflow
of new converts, most from catechized youth, the harvests
tended to be concentrated in explosive periods of revival. In
time, expectations came to match realities. No one planned it
that way. Ministers and parents suffered agonies because of it.
But by 1800 it seemed increasingly rare that young people
moved, logically, from catechism to an experiential sense of
regeneration. They lagged, held back, as if waiting for an ex-
plosion. Then, as if to break a logjam, youth of varying ages
might all move into the church within a few months, possibly
in the aftermath of a single summer communion season. Parents accommodated this pattern, and as their children moved
through the turbulent teen years they anxiously waited and
watched for signs of a glorious summer harvest, one that they
often also desired for purely personal reasons. Such a revival
might deepen their own faith, bring them a fuller certainty of
their own salvation, and above all lead to moments of unri-
valed joy and happiness. The context of guilt, of personal anxiety, and of agonizing concern for wayward youth are all illustrated in a series of revivals that began in Virginia in 1787, the
first of such scope or intensity among Presbyterians following
the American Revolution.

The minister most involved in the first of the new revivals

was John Blair Smith, who was part of the family-like circle of Scotch-Irish Presbyterian ministers. His father, Robert Smith, had immigrated from Ulster to eastern Pennsylvania. Personally converted by the preaching of Whitefield, Robert Smith studied at Samuel Blair's academy, married Blair's sister, and at a thoroughly Irish congregation at Pecua, Pennsylvania, opened his own academy. There he taught David Caldwell. His son, John Blair Smith, was able to attend the new Presbyterian College of New Jersey, taking his baccalaureate in 1773 under John Witherspoon, the eminent president who came from Scotland and finally ended the early mortality among Princeton's heads. As a student at Princeton just before the Revolution, John participated in a student revival that helped propel almost half the members of his class into the ministry. In 1775, before ordination, he became an assistant to his brother, Samuel Stanhope Smith, in the new academy that matured into Hampden-Sydney in Farmville, Virginia. As a tutor, he successfully struggled through the tests leading to ordination by 1779. When his brother moved to a chair in and later the presidency of Princeton, John took over as head of Hampden-Sydney, and as expected became a pastor of nearby congregations. Although reasonably successful as a college administrator, he was even more talented as a preacher. He had the rare ability to combine scholarship and erudition with a tender, even passionate, and quite popular mode of delivery. But after the war even he had little success in his ministry in a period that everyone characterized as dull and lifeless. In 1787, by his judgment, not one of his eighty college students was "serious and thoughtful" about religion, while some were even contemptuous of the church.

All this sounds very familiar. Smith wanted to reverse the trend. He urged elders to form prayer circles or societies in his congregations, and these soon met frequently to pray for revival. Not surprisingly the first effect was on the participants. By the summer of 1787, a few of the students, home for summer in their awakening congregations or exposed to a new wave of fervent Baptist and Methodist revivals, experienced conversion. A handful of such aroused students seemed to be the needed catalyst, and thus in the fall a revival swept through the college. Smith and his assistants provided the needed preaching. Before the year was out, students were taking the good news back to home congregations, and as always the telling of the story proved the single most powerful stimulus to local revivals. By 1788, almost all the Presbyterian congregations in southern Virginia were affected. The news of the Hampden-Sydney revivals attracted visitors both from Carolina and the Shenandoah Valley of Virginia, and thus the revival slowly spread to these areas during the next three years. By the summer of 1788, Smith exhausted himself in attending and preaching at scattered communion services, which remained the principal institutional base of almost all the revivals outside the college. Although Baptists reported successful revivals, and the Methodists were struggling with some success to form circuits, as yet we have no evidence of any ecumenical communion services.[15]

All the patterns of revival lay revealed in the spread of the Hampden-Sydney phenomenon. In the valley, around Lexington, one of the founders of Liberty Hall (later Washington College), William Graham, was struggling to develop his new college. In the typical pattern, Graham descended from Ulster-born parents who first settled in Pennsylvania. After a classical beginning in an academy conducted by James Finley, he matriculated at Princeton in the same class as John B. Smith. Before his ordination he began the long, frustrating effort that led eventually to Liberty Hall, at first simply another local Presbyterian academy (David Rice, the first Presbyterian minister to settle in Kentucky, was an early pupil, as was Samuel Doak, the pioneer Presbyterian educator in east Tennessee). In 1782 his academy gained a state charter. A later gift from George Washington led to the name Washington

15. Foote, *Sketches of Virginia* 1:408–438.

College. A passionate man, Graham gained fame for his completely extemporaneous sermons (most Presbyterian ministers still wrote them in their entirety) and for his emphasis on good hymn singing (he engaged a singing teacher, probably the first in any Presbyterian congregation).

In August 1789 Graham came, by invitation, to the Hampden-Sydney area, ostensibly to participate in a large communion service. He actually came, with several students, to observe the revivals in full climax. He hoped his young people would be moved by the fervor. They were. And Graham contributed some of the most effective sermons. Eventually, another group of about thirty young visitors from back home, predominantly well-chaperoned young women, joined in some of these later communion services. Graham, accompanied by a local minister and with all these youth in tow, returned to the valley, the mountains echoing their "songs of praise."

As so often happened, local citizens gathered in large numbers to hear wonderful accounts from Graham and his youth. Within days a revival was in full swing in neighboring congregations. In the next year it spread to all the valley, rivaling in scope, in intensity, and in the solemnity of great communions what had begun two years earlier in southern Virginia. In the midst of all this awakening, John B. Smith, by then acknowledged as the father of a great revival, came to the valley. In the Lexington area he debated with a group of Scottish seceders (the Associate Church), who always opposed the more passionate preaching and the bodily exercises that marked what to them seemed horribly undisciplined services. All the ministers most involved in the Logan County revival of 1797–1801 had some association with these previous revivals of 1787–90, revivals which seemed to diminish rapidly in the notoriously slack early nineties.[16]

Almost immediately influenced by the Hampden-Sydney

16. Ibid., 439–89.

revivals were the nearby ministers in North Carolina, including Caldwell and Craighead. The new ingredient was the sermons of James McGready, the father of the great revival in the West. McGready too derived from Ulster parents in Pennsylvania. When he was very young, his parents moved to Guilford County as part of the migration that led to David Caldwell's academy. There he grew up, gaining his grammar school education with Caldwell. We know little about his youth or his early commitment to the ministry. Perhaps because of family contacts, he returned to Pennsylvania for college and seminary instruction at the third embryonic regional Presbyterian college, an academy at Cannonsburg (later Jefferson College), near Pittsburgh, which was at the heart of another thriving Scotch-Irish empire. Licensed in the local Redstone Presbytery, McGready soon decided to return to Carolina. He stopped briefly at Hampden-Sydney during the great revival, but then only as an observer. He accepted his first pulpit at an older North Carolina congregation, in about 1790, and quickly gained fame for the careful two-day preparation that went into each of his written sermons, for his effective preaching (he almost memorized his sermons), and for his intense moral seriousness. He touched people by his prayers and sermons, and at the same time troubled them by his denunciations of anything less than perfect holiness in conduct. In some ways his style resembled that of Jonathan Edwards, but he did not possess the philosophical skills of Edwards. He soon married a Pennsylvania woman and seemed permanently settled in Guilford County. He frequently visited Caldwell's nearby academy, particularly during the height of the revivals in North Carolina around 1790, and was most welcome because of his sermons, which led to conversions and a revival-like atmosphere among the students. It seems that McGready's pulpit style was very different from that of the mild, reasonable Caldwell.[17]

17. Foote, *Sketches of North Carolina*, 367–99.

McGready's preaching also helped stimulate the zeal of a young prospective minister, William Hodge, then a student of Caldwell's. Hodge soon became a virtual protégé of Mc-Gready and was almost as effective in the pulpit. Another of Caldwell's students much influenced by McGready's preaching was Barton W. Stone, later the host minister at Cane Ridge in 1801. Notably, Stone also took a trip up to Virginia to hear John B. Smith, and then as a Presbyterian licentiate studied divinity under William Hodge. The interconnections, the family-like network, thus persisted.[18]

In 1796 McGready and a colleague, William McGee (both a student and a parishioner of David Caldwell's), were the first two ministers to respond to appeals from distant settlers along the Kentucky-Tennessee border. John Rankin, also a former member of one of David Caldwell's congregations in Guilford County, followed them west late in 1796. They were not the first Presbyterian ministers in the Cumberland area. Thomas Craighead, Caldwell's brother-in-law who eventually became a determined opponent of revival excesses, was already in Nashville, and the elderly Terah Templin, one of the pioneer ministers in Kentucky, pastored a small congregation in southern Kentucky. Neither met the religious needs of the new immigrants from North Carolina. McGee moved to a large congregation (Shiloh) in Sumner County in Tennessee, and Rankin to another congregation (the Ridge) in the same county. McGready accepted a call to three small churches just across the border in Logan County, Kentucky. Because of his missionary zeal, conflict within one of his North Carolina congregations, and the fact that his close friends had already settled in Logan County, the move must have seemed more of an opportunity, both spiritually and professionally, than a risk to McGready. William Hodge would follow him within two years, and late in 1800 a mild, already sickly minister from a Caldwell congregation in Guil-

18. Barton W. Stone, *A Short History of the Life of Barton W. Stone, Written by Himself,* in *Voices from Cane Ridge,* comp. and ed. Rhodes Thompson (St. Louis: Bethany, 1954), 36–40.

ford County, William McAdow, would settle in southern Logan County, completing the set of five "wild men" of the Cumberland. William McGee, significantly, was soon joined in the West by his brother John, another of Caldwell's students and a pioneer Methodist minister who formed an early circuit in middle Tennessee.

McGready provided the catalyst of revival in the West. He was a master at the game, having honed his skills back in North Carolina. He never fit the stereotype of a wild, ranting revivalist. His carefully written, powerful sermons were keyed to the Pauline scheme of salvation. Tall, a bit ungainly, given to plain dress, but with a powerful voice, he must have seemed like a prophet, an often angry Micah, to his audiences. Almost forbiddingly serious and grave, he could conclude his careful, logical sermons with tender and moving exhortations. But, morally austere, he condemned all worldly vices. Few lived up to his expectations. He placed almost impossible demands on his congregations, both in the depth of their self-examination and in the purity of their lives. No one ever challenged the sincerity of his own religious convictions or his complete dedication to his ministry. He wrote little save his sermons, and except for the revivals of 1797–1801 gained little fame. Yet because of placement or personality, he played a vital role in American religious history. His influence is almost beyond calculation.

Half of our detailed knowledge of the exciting events in Logan County after 1797 comes directly from McGready. He wrote down his terse "Narrative" and sent it, or abbreviated versions of it, in letters to several friends. A short version appeared in several eastern evangelical magazines, and the full narrative in the new Presbyterian-sponsored *Western Missionary Magazine* published in Pittsburgh. In one version or another it circulated throughout the country. No simple description of religious events, save possibly Jonathan Edward's *Faithful Narrative,* had as profound and lasting an effect. Even Bishop Francis Asbury, in his laborious travels to all the annual conferences of the Methodist Episcopal Church, found that, when too ill or tired to give a sermon, he could read one of McGready's letters to excellent effect. It had more influence than any sermon.[19]

When McGready arrived in Logan County in 1796, he came close to that ever mythical, ever retreating frontier. Except for a few trappers, the area of Kentucky south and west of the Barron River remained unsettled by whites until the close of the Revolution, when the area opened to land claims and settlement by veterans. Fortunately, the area contained excellent soil, some in a prairie state because of frequent burnings. The first decade of settlement was chaotic, with few original families remaining in the area, and with numerous reports of lawlessness and vigilante justice as well as Indian warfare. But by 1795, with land open to all, a new generation of permanent settlers moved in, with families and a desire to create stable communities. The North Carolina Scotch-Irish were of this type, and thus their efforts to form churches and their pleas for ministers to supply them. McGready arrived just as these families became dominant in a shrinking but settled Logan County, a county with over 5,000 people by the census of 1800.[20]

McGready took over three infant congregations named after local rivers—Red, Muddy, and Gasper. These extended from near the Tennessee line, only forty miles north of the small but booming town of Nashville, to the Gasper River set-

19. James McGready, "A Short Narrative of the Revival of Religion in Logan County," *Western Missionary Magazine* 1 (February 1803): 27–28; (March 1803): 45–54; (April 1803): 99–103; (June 1803): 172–73. McGready sent a part of this narrative in the form of a letter to Samuel Ramsey, who published it in the *New York Missionary Magazine* 3 (1802): 156–59. The same account, "Narrative of the Commencement and Progress of the Revival of 1800," October 23, 1801, is in *The Posthumous Works of the Reverend and Pious James McGready,* ed. James Smith, 2 vols. (Lousiville, Ky.: n.p., 1831), 1:ix–xvi. Francis Asbury refers to the narrative in his journal, *The Journal and Letters of Francis Asbury,* 3 vols. (Nashville: Abingdon, 1958), 2:310, although Asbury may actually have read to his congregations a letter from McGready to Dr. Thomas Coke, n.d., in *Methodist Magazine* 26 (1803): 181–84.

20. Ted Ownby, "The Logan County, Kentucky Religious Revival, 1797–1805" (senior honors thesis, Vanderbilt University, 1982), 1–11.

tlements well to the northeast of the present county seat of Russellville. McGready reported what other ministers throughout the West noted—general religious unconcern and laxity. The available evidence bears out this description. For example, the two earliest Methodist circuit preachers in Kentucky had great success in the late eighties. They gave accounts of stirring revivals, with plenty of swooning and shouting, massive conversions, and also frequent and equally dramatic experiences of sanctification (an achievement of holiness through the baptism of the Holy Spirit, all tied to a peculiar Wesleyan doctrine of perfection). In McGready's Cumberland district, a Methodist itinerant, James Haw, who joined the Presbyterians during McGready's revivals, reported 112 conversions and 47 sanctifications in the revival season of 1788. Yet from 1792, when the revivals all but ended, until 1800, a period during which Kentucky's population more than doubled, the total number of Methodists dropped by sixty-seven.[21]

As soon as he arrived in Kentucky, McGready began preparing his congregations for a revival. He stressed an experiential or sensible religion, adhered to but did not emphasize election or predestination, recommended a day of prayer and fasting each month, and made the best possible use of the customary four-day Scottish communion service. Since he pastored three widely scattered congregations, he so timed the communions that members of each small congregation could travel to each one by horseback or wagon, thus creating the critical mass of people needed for a fervent revival. The travel, the home hospitality, the break from normal routines, the all-day and, often, almost all-night services also created a special atmosphere. Finally, for people separated for years, some as long as a decade, from beloved churches and ministers, even from weekly worship services, the old, traditional communion must have represented a special type of spiritual homecoming.

21. Albert H. Redford, *The History of Methodism in Kentucky,* 3 vols. (Nashville: Southern Methodist Publishing House, 1868), 1:46–47, 249.

McGready could exploit a sense of religious depredation, yearning, and guilt.[22]

McGready began preparing his congregation in the first winter of 1796–97. By spring he noted a brief awakening at Gasper River, triggered by the spiritual experiences and confessions of one woman. Nothing untoward happened the rest of that year, but a great revival began in 1798. In that year, John Rankin moved to Logan County and took over the Gasper River congregation, which soon constructed a new meetinghouse a few miles south of the primitive one served earlier by McGready. In a series of joyous summer and fall communion seasons, first at Gasper River, then at Muddy and Red rivers, all the congregants seemed to awaken and to have no concern except religion as a harvest of converts began among the young people. But then an older, antirevivalist Presbyterian, James Balch, came and spoke out against McGready's doctrines and methods. McGready too easily blamed the cessation of the revivals in the fall on this opposition. But the magic resumed at the communion services the next summer. As McGready later noted, the extended meetings and extreme physical exercises (groaning, swooning, crying) came after the communion was over, usually at the Monday thanksgiving services. Nothing so far marred the solemnity of the sacrament.[23]

The climax of the Logan County revival came in 1800, the last year of the century. The news of the excitement had spread far and wide. Hundreds, possibly a thousand, people came from all the local churches, including those in nearby Tennessee. McGready's fist communion of the season was in June at Red River, hard on the Tennessee line, at a small log meetinghouse that measured only twenty-eight by forty feet.

22. McGready, *Posthumous Works.* These sermons, written over a lifetime, reveal McGready's doctrinal outlook; they do not reveal his pulpit style or suggest his effectiveness in the revival. Such carefully written texts provided him a theme for numerous sermons, but left him plenty of room for analysis and for contextually determined perorations or exhortations.

23. McGready, "A Short Narrative."

There, in numbers never before observed by McGready, dozens were struck down in the first massive fallings in the West. The services extended into Tuesday. Several seemed to experience rebirth (McGready, like all Presbyterian ministers, was guarded in his estimates of numbers).

The 1800 communion at Red River began an ecumenical tradition. John McGee, William McGee's Methodist brother, attended and preached at such a communion for the first time. The role of John gave the Methodists a special claim to the great revival. As John McGee later remembered the sacrament, he provided the needed spark. In the early preaching, he joined his brother and Hodge in the pulpit and, by his account, preached with much more animation and effect than the more reserved Presbyterians. Then on Monday, the final day, he gave not only the most affecting sermon of the communion, but at the very end, after the tired Presbyterian ministers had all left the meetinghouse even as the people lingered, McGee,

The reconstructed Red River meetinghouse in Logan County, Kentucky. On these grounds, in June, 1800, dozens of people swooned at a great Presbyterian communion, or the beginnings of the massive fallings in the West.

moved by the Spirit, rose and in typically Methodist fashion exhorted from the heart, moving in tears and with frequent shouts through the congregation. This wild, extemporaneous preaching was indeed alien to the Presbyterian ministers. It had its expected effect, and soon dozens were slain, lying comatose on the floor. McGee, with little modesty, referred later to this event as the beginning of the great revival, a revival that was largely Methodist in style and inspiration. But beyond the exaggeration, a crucial fact had already become apparent—the Methodists did it better and enjoyed it more. If Presbyterians were to compete, they had to move toward the Methodist style, and possibly toward the Arminian doctrines that lay behind it.[24]

In July, an eagerly awaited second sacrament at Rankin's new Gasper River meetinghouse drew people from distances of "even a hundred miles." When Rankin came to the meetinghouse for the opening Friday session, he was astonished to find from twenty to thirty wagons, with provisions, already encamped on the rising ground to the west and south of the meetinghouse, which was by the river. Clearly, the numbers were outgrowing the resources of home hospitality. The nearby houses and barns may have been inadequate for the crowds. But this possibility may not explain the families who made the individual decision to come prepared to stay on the grounds. By then, the action tended to peak in the late evening or even deep into the night. They did not want to miss it. By necessity, the preaching was mostly from the outdoor tent, in the old Scottish tradition. But the tables were set within the small meetinghouse, necessitating several servings of tables on Sunday. At least four ministers (McGee, McGready, Rankin, and Hodge) and up to seven or eight congregations participated in this soon famous sacrament. The visiting ministers had already examined their own parishioners, and probably issued their own lead tokens to those who desired to com-

24. John McGee to Thomas L. Douglas, June 23, 1820, in Redford, *History of Methodism in Kentucky*, 1:267–72.

Now a cow pasture, this is the historic "rising ground" on which over twenty families en-camped with wagons at an extended communion in July, 1800. The Gasper River meet-inghouse was along the river where the trees are in the background, and where now only a cemetery survives.

mune. The ministers rotated the duties—the preaching of pre-paratory sermons, the institution and fencing of the tables, the serving of the bread and wine. While some served tables, oth-ers preached from the tent.

The Gasper River sacrament of 1800 became famous. John Rankin, the host minister, traveled back through east Tennes-see and on to his former congregation in North Carolina. His account helped spark the first great awakening among Pres-byterians in east Tennessee and in Carolina. The number of wagons on the grounds at Gasper River, and the informal tents created around some of the wagons, also gave Gasper River a disputed but persuasive claim to being the first camp meeting in America. By most later images of camps, it scarcely qualified; there had been no planning, no tents or cab-ins, no regulations. And it was far from the first occasion when distant visitors had stayed at least overnight at communions, Baptist associations, or Methodist conferences. It is possible, as later claimed, that some had camped a month earlier at Red River. But having said all this, one has to acknowledge the enduring significance of Gasper River, of what flowed from the uncoordinated choices of a few families. The news of what happened at Gasper spread like wildfire, and the idea of camping seemed almost immediately to capture the imagination of Christians from New England to Louisiana, particularly those caught up in the new wave of revivals. Within a mere two years, organized camps became commonplace, and the camp meeting was on its way to becoming a vital new institution. Methodists, who adopted it most enthusiastically, refuted charges that it was not scriptural by noting that the tents or arbors made it the Christian equivalent of the Jewish Feast of Tabernacles.[25]

Gasper River was only an early climax. Nothing, save possibly the camping out, began there. Nothing ended. According to McGready, his final summer sacrament, at Muddy River, close to Russellville, equaled or exceeded that at Gasper. But these sacraments joined at least eight others in both Logan County and nearby Tennessee. At least seven ministers and their congregations hosted communions, which were so scheduled that no two fell on the same weekend. By this stage the congregations seemed to be competing in the planning of such sacraments. At Muddy River members of the congregation spread straw and sewed together sheets to accommodate campers. In this first great wave of exciting sacraments, even ministers who later opposed revival excesses participated— perhaps in a sense had to participate, for the outbreaks accompanied the normal, scheduled communion services. Even Thomas Craighead, who was later tossed out of the Presbyterian church for his rationalism, joined enthusiastically in a sacrament in Sumner County, where two of his daughters were

25. John Rankin, "Autobiography," a manuscript in Shaker Book A, Kentucky Museum, Western Kentucky University, 18–19; Theophilus Arminius (an obvious pseudonym), "Account of the Rise and Progress of the Work of God in the Western Country," *Methodist Magazine* 2 (May 1819): 186.

possibly converted, and then hosted a large sacrament in Nashville, one with an estimated forty conversions. The largest communion of all may have been that hosted by the Shiloh church in Sumner County, in a communion held at nearby Deshas Creek (to be near the water needed for horses and campers), where McGready recorded seventy possible conversions. His first protégé, William Hodge, had just become minister of this largest congregation in middle Tennessee.[26]

Although the focus, and national attention, shifted to central Kentucky in 1801, the great communions continued in the Cumberland area. If anything the number, and the fervor, increased in 1801. Probably in 1802 McGready wrote a second letter, announcing the continuing work, rejoicing in the apparent conversion of his three daughters, and reporting the amazing effects on Negroes and children, who exhorted wonderfully. In a claim that eclipsed that of any reported revival in American history, he judged authentic the conversion of a three-year-old child.[27]

By the fall of 1800, less-advertised sacramental services in east Tennessee and in the Piedmont of North Carolina possibly rivaled or even exceeded, in size if not in exercises, those in the Cumberland area. By then the greatest revival in American history was in full swing. All its perplexities, all its internal paradoxes, would come to a head at Cane Ridge in the next summer. But one must remark that little if anything that happened in this great revival was new, without precedents that stretched back through two centuries, to Carolina, to Virginia, to Pennsylvania, and ultimately to Ulster and Scotland. The heritage lived on, and not without a keen awareness on the part of McGready and all the older ministers. They knew the legends about the great sacraments at Cambuslang. None of their communions, not even Cane Ridge, rivaled those in size and probably not in fervor.

26. Ownby, "Logan County Religious Revival," 21–22; William Hodge to Francis Asbury, n.d., *Methodist Magazine* 26 (1803): 268–72.

27. McGready to the editors of the *Western Missionary Magazine* 1 (June 1803): 176–77 (the letter bears the impossible date of July 26, 1803).

CHAPTER TWO

The Cane Ridge Communion

As at Cambuslang in 1742, the great communion at Cane Ridge in central Kentucky in August 1801 did not begin but climaxed an intense religious revival. No one can explain this revival, in the sense of citing a set of sufficient conditions for it. The one most likely necessary condition was the well-advertised success of James McGready and his colleagues in Logan County in the preceding three summers.

In the spring of 1801 a great religious excitement spread over the beautiful, lush bluegrass area of central Kentucky. This fertile area, literally a land of milk and honey for farmers who moved from the thin soils of the Piedmont, was first settled by whites just before the Revolution. It boomed in the 1790s, moving from a near-frontier area to a reasonably settled, stable, and prospering region, soon to be the most productive agricultural area in the United States. By 1800 the state of Kentucky (which was admitted to the Union in 1792) had over 220,000 people, with the heaviest concentration in the central counties. The surge of growth had outpaced the formation of new churches, leaving probably half of all Kentuckians outside any organized congregations (formal membership was not much above 10 percent). This lag joined with the coldness, religious indifference, or religious rationalism noted by almost all ministers in the nineties.

Despite the widespread but imprecise descriptions of rationalists and deists by frustrated ministers, most Kentucky settlers retained at least a modicum of Christian belief. However busy or distracted, most still understood, and when challenged still responded to, the Pauline scheme of salvation. They knew the meaning of sinfulness, feared damnation however they understood it, and suffered intense guilt if they departed from what they believed to be Christian moral standards. Above all, many yearned for the heightened religious experience, for the warmth of communal support and the exhilaration of communion services, that they remembered from their youth or from earlier waves of revival. Finally, a solid nucleus of faithful Christians, often parents, suffered all the generational anxieties that had fueled the revivals of 1787–90. They sorrowed for their young people, most of whom seemed indifferent to religion.

Another possible factor does not yield to any evidence. The transition to a new century might have triggered a renewed concern about religion or inspired millenarian speculation. Yet ministers noted little significance in the date and did not emphasize it in their preaching, although evangelical journals did carry a few articles about the new century. Millenarian hopes did soar in 1801, but seemingly much more as a product than a cause of the revivals. Equally inconclusive were factors in the larger society. Insecurities had always abounded in the western country. Even as the threat from Indians lessened, numerous families faced the loss of farms because of contested or overlapping land claims. But these problems were not noticeably worse in 1801 than in preceding years.

Equally problematical was the influence of the frontier. This purported factor has so pervaded the scholarship on western revivals as to become a truism. The trouble is that this explanation lacks clarity and, when broken down into clear propositions, seems largely mistaken or false. No word is more elusive than *frontier*. In a literal sense, no revivals took place, or could take place, among the first scattered white settlers in any area of the West. Revivals always required clusters of people, enough to form churches. Some revivals, such as those in Logan County, occurred within a decade of most early white settlement and the development of new farms out of a virtual wilderness. Maybe the insecurities of moving west, of getting a new start, or the hardship and loneliness experienced by isolated families, or the cultural and material deprivations suffered by many families in the first years on a new homestead had something to do with receptivity to revivalistic religion, or at least helped shape the response to this religion. Even this thesis is hard to prove. If anything, the evidence goes against it.

The most plausible test of the frontier explanation would seem to be comparison. Were the revivals in Logan County, those demonstrably closest to the frontier, in any essentials different from those in central Kentucky, an area more populous and with families more removed, in space and time, from the insecurities of first settlement? It is difficult to cite any significant differences. Were the revivals west of the mountains essentially different from those in Virginia and North Carolina between 1787 and 1790, or even those in central Virginia in the 1740s? This is a more difficult question. The few innovations in the West seem either a matter of context, as in the first reported camping on the grounds, or the outcome of a process of normal elaboration, as in the case of the slightly larger repertoire of physical exercises. The Kentucky revivals paralleled a new wave east of the mountains, revivals likewise triggered by McGready's narrative about Logan County or by the early reports of events in central Kentucky. Were these eastern expressions of this great revival essentially different from those in central Kentucky? Not clearly so. Reports from North Carolina, South Carolina, and Georgia in 1801, and from western Virginia and Pennsylvania in 1802, are so similar to those from Kentucky in 1801 as to suggest plagiarism. Within a year the camping spread east. The same physical exercises occurred. It is true that a few Presbyterian apologists in the East tried to make good their private hopes that their revivals were not quite as wild as those in the caricatured West. They first launched the myth of frontier exceptionalism, a myth that contained, in almost all subsequent literature, the false hypothesis that the families that moved west somehow reverted, or regressed, to a more primitive or ignorant or superstitious stage of civilization. This then joined with other established, and almost completely false, assertions that either the revivals themselves, or at least the more extreme physical exercises, attracted only an especially ignorant and backward subclass of society.

Religious stirrings began in central Kentucky during the winter of 1800–1801. Reports of such ferment came from all areas and from all evangelical ministers, whether Presbyterian, Methodist, or Baptist. It is impossible to cite any one opening event, although from several parochial vantage points individuals developed coherent scenarios about the origin and progress of a great revival. Not surprisingly, all gave priority to their own denomination. The Baptists, without massive crowds, interdenominational cooperation, or extreme bodily exercises, enjoyed unprecedented revivals throughout the winter of 1800–1801. The Elkhorn Association, around Lexington, reported numerous conversions and baptisms each month. Some congregations gained over 100 converts, including several blacks. The Baptists reported 10,000 converts in the state for the year, an unbelievable figure that, had it been correct, would have meant a tripling of Baptist membership.[1]

The Methodists not only claimed priority in 1800 in Logan County, but dated the beginnings of the revival in central Kentucky to a quarterly conference of the Hinkstone Circuit, near Lexington. There, in early June, William McKendree, the greatest leader of western Methodism, a participant in several of the Cumberland revivals a year earlier, and a later bishop, preached a key sermon. Neighboring Presbyterian ministers

1. *Gospel News, or a Brief Account of the Revival of Religion in Kentucky and Several Other Parts of the United States* (Baltimore: n.p., 1801), 1–3.

joined McKendree in the meeting. By the Methodist interpretation, the revival then spread to nearby Presbyterian churches and to the sacramental occasions, which were soon enlivened by Methodist preaching.[2]

Of course the Presbyterians knew better. They could report several fervent Presbyterian sacraments that predated the Hinkstone conference, although not necessarily the protracted meetings in Baptist churches. In fact, everyone was correct, at least in part. All simply offered a local perspective on a religious phenomenon that was much more general than they knew. Revivals, of somewhat variant types, seemed to be popping up not only all over Kentucky but all over the United States in 1801. Leading eastern evangelical journals received an avalanche of glowing revival reports from ministers all over the country, from New England and Yale University to the mid-Atlantic states, the South, and the West. Yet, for reasons that are unclear, the best attended and most explosive almost always involved Presbyterian communions. Among these, Cane Ridge was the largest and soon, by far, the best known and most influential.[3]

The Cane Ridge communion marked the climax, not the end, of the most exciting communion season in the history of American Presbyterianism. From May to November at least fifty congregations in Kentucky held their scheduled four-day communions. At least twenty of these predated Cane Ridge, although only a dozen or so in central Kentucky were directly linked to Cane Ridge. As in Scotland, the greatest communions came in the midst, not at the beginning, of such revivals. In the months before Cane Ridge more and more church mem-

2.   Albert H. Redford, *The History of Methodism in Kentucky*, 3 vols. (Nashville: Southern Methodist Publishing House, 1868), 1:351–56.

3.   The scope of the revivals is borne out by reports in the *Connecticut Evangelical Magazine*, the *New York Missionary Magazine and Repository of Religious Intelligence*, and in three books that heralded the revivals: *Surprising Accounts of the Revival of Religion, in the United States of America* (Philadelphia: Woodward, 1802); *Gospel News;* and most extensively in *Increase of Piety, or the Revival of Religion in the United States of America* (Newburyport, Conn.: Angier March, 1802).

bers became intensely concerned about their salvation, large numbers of youth or unchurched adults fell under deep conviction of sinfulness, increased numbers of people flocked to all types of religious services, and a growing stream of people reported all the expected signs of conversion. The most intense religious experiences, the most agonizing despair and the most ecstatic joy, seemed to be reserved for the communion season. It was then that most youth suffered the deepest conviction and moved toward the relief or comfort that marked conversion.

But the success of a communion depended on a prior buildup of religious concern and excitement through weekly worship services or, increasingly, through what Presbyterians called societies or socials. These had distant roots in Scottish Presbyterianism, particularly among the old Covenanters (the Reformed Church), and close parallels in the Moravian and Methodist denominations. The socials provided a functional substitute among Presbyterians for the much-imitated Methodist class system, and they anticipated later weekly prayer meetings or even aspects of Sunday schools. These societies often met in homes, including that of the minister. The focus was on fellowship, prayer, and personal testimony. In some Presbyterian congregations ministers used these society meetings to examine applicants and to award communion tokens. Such societies provided a voice, and leadership roles, for those normally excluded from active participation in worship— women, children, slaves. As revival specialists soon realized, such preparatory meetings were an indispensable prelude to a successful revival or, in the Presbyterian case, a fulfilling communion season. Even during the Cane Ridge communion, at least one society meeting took place in a nearby private home.

One center of revival by the spring of 1801 was Bourbon County, in the lush agricultural district to the east of Lexington. It was there that Barton W. Stone was to play a critical role. According to his often fallible memoir, written long after the event, Stone decided in early May of 1801 to visit his old colleagues, James McGready and John Rankin, at Gasper River, there to participate in and observe firsthand one of the by then famous communion services, in which several families camped on the grounds. He returned home to tell his story at his two churches, Cane Ridge and Concord. His congregations eagerly awaited him. As so often before, the telling of the story led to an almost immediate eruption of physical exercises roughly similar to those he described. Multitudes collected at Cane Ridge for his first regular Sunday appointment; most went home weeping. At the evening preaching at Concord, much more extreme physical exercises erupted. On Monday Stone attended a society meeting in the home of a church member, one marked by intense interest, extended testimonies, and the conversion of a leading citizen of the Cane Ridge community. It was at this meeting that several of the people swooned. Following Stone's return came the regular communion season at Concord, in late May, just before Stone again left the area to get married. This five-day communion fully duplicated those back in Logan County, with not only neighboring Presbyterians but also Methodists attending. By now, several families participated in every communion close enough for convenient attendance as the excitement mounted toward a climax at Cane Ridge in August.[4]

The experience of two individuals illustrates the effect of such intensifying religious excitement. Colonel Robert Patterson of Lexington, one of Kentucky's leading citizens, a famed Indian fighter and militia captain, one of the founders of Lexington, and a longtime patron of the Lexington Presbyterian Church, attended and wrote descriptions of at least eight sacraments during the summer of 1801. Historians are indebted to him for one of the more careful and believable descriptions of the Cane Ridge revival. John Lyle, the newly arrived minister

4. John Carr, *Early Times in Middle Tennessee* (Nashville: n.p., 1857), 39; Barton W. Stone, *A Short History of the Life of Barton W. Stone*, in James R. Rogers, *The Cane Ridge Meeting House, to Which is Appended the Autobiography of B. W. Stone* (Cincinnati: Standard Publishing House, 1910), 153–58.

of the Salem congregation, near Paris, also kept a detailed diary of the sacraments that he attended during that hectic summer of 1801.

From his perspective in Lexington, Patterson believed the revival began in early May at a sacrament on the Licking, northeast of Lexington. He did not attend this communion. The next notable sacrament he reported was at Cabin Creek near the Ohio River in the third week of May (the communion day was May 22). This communion was in the congregation of Richard McNemar and was arguably the first that exhibited all the exercises that occurred at Cane Ridge. Since McNemar was a former elder in the Cane Ridge congregation, as many Cane Ridge parishioners as could manage traveled the difficult fifty miles to take part. The communion had enduring significance for the career of McNemar and for the subsequent New Light or Christian movement and even for Shaker success in the West. At the Cabin Creek sacrament a reported fifty or sixty people fell (McNemar told of carrying these to a part of the meetinghouse and laying them out in squares), although such a display was mild compared to some of the exercises later reported and encouraged by McNemar.

The first communion attended by Patterson was at Concord on the next weekend. It followed a society meeting at Cane Ridge on Friday, which he also attended. He was becoming a connoisseur of such communions, and began tabulating the results. At Concord, opponents protested for the first time; the meetings went on continually, day and night; untypically, the communion tables were set outdoors before the tent in a grove of beech trees; 250 communed out of 4,000 present; and 12 families brought provisions and camped on the grounds, a possible first for central Kentucky. Patterson was at the Stony Creek sacrament in early June with his family (40 wagons encamped, 8,000 people, 250 who fell), and then remained at home for the Lexington communion in late June, having to miss a larger one at Indian Creek (a famous communion, with a reported 10,000 present, 50 wagons, and 800 "slain"). Patterson stayed home in July, possibly did some work, but resumed his pilgrimage at Cane Ridge, and followed this by smaller sacraments at Paris, Walnut Hill, Beaver, and Blue Springs before writing his report in late September.[5]

Lyle began his diary with the sacrament at his Salem church on June 18. He was especially moved during the serving of the tables, and noted the first person to fall, a woman who breathed hard, "like a sheep down on a hot day." On the third Sunday of June, Lyle participated at the sacrament at Lexington, the home congregation of Patterson. Only here, and later at Cane Ridge, did their paths cross. The great communion at Indian Creek on the same weekend attracted the "hotter" ministers, including McNemar and Stone, and even drew off many of the young people of Lexington. The few ministers present, in a congregation made up of many of the gentry of central Kentucky, therefore expected a calm communion. It was not. The falling began on Sunday, the first observed by many in this city congregation. Anxious observers tried various home remedies in attempts to revive those on the ground, with no success. As men and women fell, Lyle preached against enthusiasm (not against physical exercises, which seemed involuntary, but against reliance on visions and dreams). His attempt to keep order typified his subsequent role in the great sacraments, yet his preaching often helped trigger the wildest audience response, leaving him in a dilemma. His ego pushed him toward a popular pulpit style, while he worried about his own pride: "I hope I am in some measure to promote my redeemer's kingdom and not striving to be the greatest."[6]

5. "An Account of the Revival of Religion Which Began in the Eastern Part of the State of Kentucky in May, 1801," doc. 105, book 3, Robert Patterson Papers, Draper Collection, State Historical Society of Wisconsin, Madison; Colonel James Paterson [sic] to Rev. John King, September 25, 1801, in *Increase of Piety*, 35–40, and also in several other evangelical publications; Richard M'Nemar, *The Kentucky Revival, or a Short History of the Late Outpouring of the Spirit of God* (Lexington, 1808; rpt. Joplin, Mo.: College Press, n.d.), 23–24.

6. Diary of Rev. John Lyle, 16, n.d., Manuscripts Division, Kentucky Historical Society, Frankfort.

While Patterson remained home, Lyle traveled to the Pleasant Point sacrament on June 29 and there observed dozens on the ground, including men young and old. He talked to those who had fallen, trying to assess both their physical sensations and spiritual experiences. One woman fell repeatedly, week after week, out of concern not for herself but for the salvation of members of her family. She finally found comfort by resignation, by leaving it all to God. Lyle then recommended this strategy to others in distress.[7]

These accounts illustrate how the excitement built in preparation for the Cane Ridge communion. Barton Stone, in the midst of his travels, did a great job in advance publicity. He also established close working relationships with the Methodists, involving them in the planning. Stone's forte was organization and ecumenical cooperation. He had few of McGready's pulpit skills. In many ways he seemed an inappropriate host for such a historic event. He was far from the most effective preacher among his colleagues in central Kentucky. Although he preached at least twice, and exhorted frequently at the Cane Ridge sacrament, he was in no way a dominating figure. At the time he was a young and not very confident minister, only two years past ordination, and in many respects a lukewarm Presbyterian. His background in no wise prepared him for Cane Ridge or gave any hint that he would occupy a strategic position in the great revival, a position that involved circumstances more than talent.

Born in 1772, Stone was an almost accidental Presbyterian. His parents, of English backgound, lived in southern Maryland until his father's death in 1779, when the widow and children moved to Pittsylvania County in southern Virginia. Stone thus came into the orbit of Piedmont Presbyterianism, both in Virginia and just across the border in North Carolina. He did not grow up in a church, although his family was nominally Anglican in an area without clergy during the Revolution. Serious, bookish, young Barton attended religious ser-

7. Ibid., 1–16.

vices conducted by itinerant Baptist and Methodist preachers and, save for circumstances, might have ended up in Methodism, a denomination with doctrines as close to his own later beliefs as those of Presbyterianism. In 1790 Stone's mother and brothers provided him the means to get a classical education. Given the high reputation of David Caldwell, they sent Barton to the nearby (thirty miles) log cabin "college" just in time for him to become caught up in the revival that swept the school under the effective preaching of McGready. During a period of over a year, he there endured the agonizing self-doubts and despair that made up the usual conversion biography. In the depths of his despair he attended a communion presided over by John Blair Smith of Hampden-Sydney College, but eventually found "comfort" only after hearing a sermon by a more mild and loving William Hodge. Thus, his religious pilgrimage led him to the three most effective architects of the 1787–90 revival. Because they were Presbyterians, and because he came to understand his own personal salvation in Presbyterian terms, he committed himself to the Presbyterian ministry. After he had completed his education with Caldwell, Stone applied as a candidate for the ministry before the Orange Presbytery in 1793 and did assigned seminary work under Hodge. He would be one of the first local Presbyterian ministers whose family heritage was neither Scotch-Irish nor English Presbyterian. In this sense also he was an alien in the Presbyterian camp.[8]

According to his later memory, colored by his subsequent career, Stone began questioning certain Presbyterian doctrines prior to his ordination. Before beginning his ministerial career, he joined a brother in Oglethorpe County, Georgia, and there taught in a Methodist school in 1795–96. He remained a Presbyterian, but increased his sympathies for Methodism. In Georgia he first encountered the Republican Methodists, who by this time often called themselves simply

8. William G. West, *Barton Warren Stone: Early American Advocate of Christian Unity* (Nashville: Disciples of Christ Historical Society, 1954), 1–18.

Christians. Back in North Carolina in 1796, determined to resume his chosen vocation, he passed his examination and received a license to preach. As he remembered the trial, he was able to finesse questions about sensitive Calvinist doctrines. He at first intended to move to Florida, but instead decided to go over the mountains, where various Presbyterian congregations eagerly sought ministers. He whetted his preaching skills and gained some needed confidence in churches in southwest Virginia and east Tennessee in the summer of 1796, then crossed the Cumberland Mountains into middle Tennessee to preach in vacant congregations and to meet with old friends and colleagues from North Carolina. Only in the late fall did he move on to central Kentucky. Then he received preaching invitations from the vacant congregations of Cane Ridge and Concord, among whom were some of his friends from North Carolina. They liked his preaching, and he gained new confidence in the pulpit. But before accepting their call as pastor, he had to return to Georgia on business, and as part of his trip did fund-raising in South Carolina for a college then planned by the Transylvania Presbytery, which included all the Presbyterian congregations in Kentucky, southern Ohio, and the Cumberland area of Tennessee.

Stone returned to his two congregations in 1798, accepted their call as permanent minister, and successfully petitioned the presbytery for ordination, which took place in October. Later he contended that, in the question period, he announced his adherence to the Westminster Confession only insofar as it was consistent with the Bible. Although a few colleagues knew of his doubts about certain church doctrines, the presbytery accepted his answer. In fact, the assembled ministers apparently did not note the qualification or suspect a problem. Later they could not remember any exception on Stone's part, leading to an embarrassing controversy. It is possible that Stone exaggerated his earlier doubts, or gave more significance to his reservations, voiced or unvoiced, than was justified at the time. In any case, in 1798 he began a long, highly significant ministry to his two rather troubled congregations.[9]

Cane Ridge was an unlikely site for the historic communion of 1801. A vibrant but troubled congregation in one of the most prosperous agricultural areas of the West, it dated from only about 1790 (the records are not conclusive, although the congregation later accepted the date of 1790). The first minister, Robert Finley, one of several Presbyterian ministers to bear that prominent Irish name, was born in Bucks County, Pennsylvania, as was a close friend, Daniel Boone. Much earlier, another Finley, John, had preceded Daniel Boone into Kentucky in 1767, and led the first Boone party back again in 1769. Robert Finley graduated from Princeton. There he had worked under John Witherspoon and was a classmate of John Blair Smith of Hampden-Sydney. He then prepared himself for the ministry and, typical of almost all Princeton-trained clergy, taught the classical languages to young men in a series of schools or academies attached to his churches. At the beginning of the Revolution he served as a missionary to leaderless congregations in North Carolina, suspended his ministry to fight in the patriot cause against Cornwallis, and then returned to the ministry. In 1784 he accompanied Daniel Boone from North Carolina to central Kentucky and reconnoitered possible land for settlement in areas around what became Cane Ridge. But because of family reluctance to move west, he first preached at congregations in South Carolina before moving to the Redstone Presbytery of western Virginia and Pennsylvania. Notably, Finley seemed unable to settle permanently and typically held ministerial positions for only brief periods. This chequered history suggests the volatility, wanderlust, and possibly alcoholism that subsequently doomed his career at Cane Ridge.

Finley and a group of colonists from western Virginia migrated down the Ohio River in the year his son recalled as

9. Stone, *A Short History* in Roger, *The Cane Ridge Meeting House*, 119–47.

1788, to settle near Flemingsburg, Kentucky. Presbyterial records suggest the move may have been one or two years later. After one year, the ever restless Finley left this area to move to the familiar and fertile cane brakes of Bourbon County, there to minister to the twin congregations of Cane Ridge and Concord. Some of his Virginia parishioners apparently moved with him, but a majority of the subsequent settlers in the area came through the Cumberland Gap from North Carolina, with the most prominent from Presbyterian congregations in Iredell County. Finley already knew some of these people, who avidly sought a minister. By local legends, in 1791 Finley led the Cane Ridge congregation in erecting a plain but superbly constructed meetinghouse of uncaulked logs that measured fifty by thirty feet. Actually, the building probably preceded his arrival. The building had no window-panes, and its seats and floor were made out of smooth logs. The meetinghouse, one of the largest log churches in that

The Cane Ridge meetinghouse in 1932, after preservationists had exposed the original logs and had reassembled the original gallery.

area of Kentucky, could seat 350, accommodating up to 500 in crowded communion seasons. Its capacity depended, in large part, on a gallery or balcony that extended toward the raised side-wall pulpit from three sides, creating what amounted to a second story. Although often referred to as a slave gallery and reached by a steep outside staircase or ladder, this space was too large, and too much needed, to be restricted to blacks. The church sat at the crest of an extended ridge in a partially open area covered by native bamboo, the cane that gave the ridge its name. Its one deficiency, at least for large crowds, was a lack of water. No creeks or reliable springs are presently within a mile of the building, and old records mention only one probably small spring a half mile from the church.[10]

Finley not only preached but quickly established a typical academy at Cane Ridge. Given his Princeton degree, the academy attracted students from long distances, and in its brief three- or four-year existence served much the same role as Caldwell's log college in Guilford County. But Finley's early achievements were soon jeopardized by his inability to control his use of alcohol. As yet the temperance issue had not become prominent among Scotch-Irish Presbyterians (sensitivity to the issue followed the revivals). In 1794 few Presbyterians objected to the moderate consumption of alcohol, even by ministers. Drink was an accepted, even though soon a threatening, aspect of Scotch-Irish culture. But Finley exceeded the allowable leeway, at least by the estimate of several prominent members of his two congregations. They charged him with drunkenness before presbytery, leading to over two years of complicated procedural arguments in the Transylvania Presbytery. Finley, who was evasive and uncooperative, and who brought charges of contumacy against accusing members of his Session at Cane Ridge, finally in 1795 refused to remain under the jurisdiction of the presbytery and thus

10. Rogers, *The Cane Ridge Meeting House*, 13–38; Joseph A. Thacher, Jr., "James B. Finley: A Biography" (Ph.D. diss., University of Kentucky, 1967), 5–9.

The restored interior of the Cane Ridge meetinghouse, viewed from near the raised pulpit. The basic structure, including all the timbers, dates from 1791; however, the internal stairs and the pews are more recent.

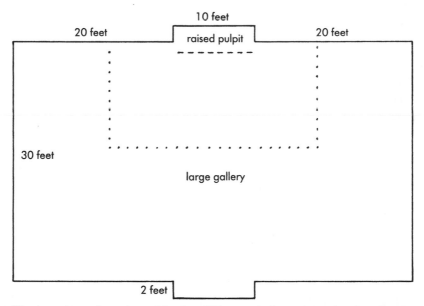

The approximate dimensions of the Cane Ridge meetinghouse. (Note that the gallery is almost a complete second story.)

avoided an open trial. The presbytery suspended him from the ministry for his refusal to conform to church order, not for his drinking. Western Presbyterians, desperate to gain able ministers, were long-suffering in their efforts to reform ministerial behavior, and continued in fellowship several penitent and cooperative ministers whose conduct was much more scandalous than Finley's.[11]

Behind this nasty conflict one senses deep divisions in the two congregations. Several families remained loyal to Finley. His opponents included those who espoused a rigorous, righteous, and affecting form of Christianity in the tradition of McGready (Richard McNemar, a prominent elder and later minister, was among Finley's accusers). Notably, some of Finley's strongest opponents became stalwarts of the church under Stone. Even as the conflict simmered, Finley characteristically began planning another move, in part motivated by problems with land titles in Kentucky. In 1795, joined by up to half of the families in his two congregations (he said 300 families), he moved north to establish a colony near Chillicothe, Ohio. Finley did not lose contact with Cane Ridge. He came back for the great communion in 1801 and preached effectively to a large outdoor gathering, but as a defrocked minister he could not officiate at the communion tables. After Finley's departure from central Kentucky, other immigrants, from North Carolina or elsewhere, moved into the Cane Ridge and Concord communities. One discerns by then the beginning of the breakdown of the earlier Scotch-Irish homogeneity in what was becoming a cultural melting pot in bluegrass Kentucky. Soon congregations would not be composed solely of friends and neighbors from communities east of the mountains.

For reasons that are not clear, the great revival of 1801 was more stormy, and more divisive, for Presbyterians than for Baptists or Methodists. By most measures, Presbyterianism

11. "Extracts from the Minutes of the Transylvania Presbytery, 1786–1837," in *The Presbyterians, 1783–1840*, vol. 2 of *Religion on the American Frontier*, ed. William Warren Sweet (New York: Harper and Brothers, 1936), 149–61.

in 1800 arguably made up the strongest denomination in Kentucky, but it would so only briefly. In the state it had approximately thirty settled ministers serving at least sixty congregations on a regular basis. All these preached occasionally, by assignment of presbytery, in almost as many emergent congregations without settled ministers. Total active membership hardly exceeded 2,000, but at least five times this many people had some tie to Presbyterian congregations. The Baptists had more ministers, more congregations, and probably more members, but unlike Presbyterians they did not have extensive educational requirements for ministers or stringent standards for recognizing new congregations. In 1800 the Methodists had only 1,741 recorded members (an honest count because of rigorous reporting rules enforced by their bishop, Francis Asbury). They came later to Kentucky, suffered internal splits in the preceding decade (the breaking off of Republican Methodism), but were well organized for rapid expansion, which came almost explosively after the great revival. Methodists had a tight episcopal organization; under a quadrennial General Conference, the church had regional annual conferences, more localized districts, and at the lowest level its effective circuits. The circuits, made up of as many as eight congregations or "stations," met in quarterly conferences, and were served by an itinerant clergy (in Kentucky one minister usually served each circuit, and none of the early circuits had more than two ministers).[12]

The Presbyterians had a head start in Kentucky because of the preponderance of Scotch-Irish pioneers, although settled Baptist ministers came along with the earliest Presbyterian missionaries. The first permanent Presbyterian minister to settle in Kentucky was David Rice, from the Shenandoah Valley in Virginia. Father Rice, as he would soon be called, settled near Danville in 1783 and within three years had helped organize three congregations. Rice, who was of Welsh-English ex-

12. John B. Boles, *Religion in Antebellum Kentucky* (Lexington: University Press of Kentucky, 1976), 5–12.

traction, came originally from Hanover County, Virginia, and was a convert of the great Davies, with whom he subsequently studied at Princeton. He married the daughter of Samuel Blair, was ordained in a church founded by Davies, but soon moved to Bedford County in the upper valley, where he remained during the Revolution. Soon after settling in Kentucky he opened an academy. A determined enemy of slavery, he served as a delegate to the Kentucky Constitutional Convention in 1792, but was unsuccessful in seeking a plan for gradual abolition. By the Cane Ridge communion he suffered from severe depression (melancholy) and was temporarily without a church, but he was still active and would be a moderate and conciliating voice in the schisms that followed the great revival.[13]

Within a year of Rice's arrival, the more controversial Adam Rankin (not related to John) moved near Lexington, establishing Presbyterianism in this population center. He eventually left the church because of his fanatical opposition to the use of Watts's hymns and founded a small Associate Synod (Seceder) congregation. These two ministers, plus two recently ordained probationers, James Crawford and Terah Templin, plus Thomas Craighead down in Nashville, in 1786 formed the Transylvania Presbytery, which embraced not only all of the future state of Kentucky but middle Tennessee and all new settlements in southern Ohio.[14]

The early Presbyterian immigrants to central Kentucky, who were predominantly from Virginia, were soon joined by another stream from North Carolina. The presbytery expanded rapidly, with new congregations and new ministers joining almost yearly. From 1795 to 1801 approximately

13. David Rice, "Memoirs of Rev. David Rice," in *An Outline of the History of the Church in the State of Kentucky,* ed. Robert H. Bishop (Lexington, Ky.: Skillman, 1824), 13–14, 51, 55, 62, 66, 77, 95.

14. Robert Davidson, *History of the Presbyterian Church in the State of Kentucky* (New York: Carter, 1847), 64, 68, 73–79, 86, 88–95.

twenty-five new ministers either moved to Kentucky (from Pennsylvania, Virginia, or North Carolina) or qualified locally for ordination. The Transylvania Presbytery relaxed normal educational requirements in order to license aspiring ministers, and thus helped meet the imperious demand for ministers. By 1798 this single western presbytery was unwieldy in both size and territory. It successfully petitioned the distant Synod of Virginia for division into three presbyteries, which the synod agreed to in 1799. One new presbytery (Washington) included northern Kentucky and southern Ohio, a second (West Lexington) the central area of Kentucky, while the redrawn borders of the Transylvania Presbytery embraced western Kentucky and middle Tennessee. In 1802, in the immediate aftermath of the great revival, the General Assembly of the church created a much-needed Synod of Kentucky.[15] But even as the new synod first convened it faced a series of crises and impending schisms. The great Cane Ridge communion had a critical role in producing the first of these crises.

During the day on Friday, August 6, 1801, people began arriving at Cane Ridge. The congregation had hosted such communions in earlier years. But it had been clear for weeks before that this would not be an ordinary summer sacrament. In this sense it closely resembled Cambuslang. By Saturday the roads were jammed with people, some strangers, some from great distances. One traveler, while still on the road, penned a prescient letter to a friend in Baltimore. He said he was on his way to the "greatest meeting, of its kind ever known." He noted that "religion has got to such a height here, that people attend from a great distance; on this occasion I doubt not but there will be 10,000 people, and perhaps 500 wagons. The people encamp on the ground, and continue

15. Ibid., 119–30; "Extracts from the Minutes of the Transylvania Presbytery," 172, 183–84.

This swale to the southwest of the Cane Ridge meetinghouse was probably the site of the
preaching tent and the largest assembly area at the great Cane Ridge revival.

praising God, day and night, for one whole week before they
break up."[16]

Much that happened was familiar. The congregation knew
the customs. Families in the church, possibly even local non–
church members, had always tried to be good hosts. It is not
clear that Stone or his parishioners did much special planning
for this communion. Ordinarily, much of the preaching took
place outdoors. Thus, either in earlier years or in preparation
for the expected extra visitors in 1801, the congregation had
built its tent, the covered lecture platform or stage about 100
yards to the southwest of the meetinghouse. Whether they
also spread straw or arranged log seats is not clear. Probably
they did not, since none of over a dozen firsthand reports refer
to anything more than the traditional tent. In any case, it is
clear that the congregation did not construct facilities for

16. Letter from Bourbon County to a friend in Baltimore, August 7, 1801, in *Gospel
News,* 4, and in slightly different form in *Methodist Magazine* 25 (1802): 263.

would-be campers. Stone later remembered that members of the congregation brought food, and spread it on long tables (undoubtedly the portable tables used for communion on Sunday), and then invited neighbors to share. But only a miracle like that of the loaves and fishes could have so expanded local supplies as to meet the total needs of the overwhelming number of visitors. Soon both food and fodder ran short, forcing many families to cut short their stay at Cane Ridge.

Undoubtedly normal home hospitality accommodated most of the neighboring families who customarily attended the Cane Ridge sacrament. More affluent hosts might take in three or four such families, but much of the hospitality must have been spartan. Children and even adults had to sleep on the floor or in barns. A dozen people might sleep, with no privacy, in a single room in a small log cabin. Wives joined in preparing meals, many cooked and eaten outdoors. From sources outside the Cane Ridge congregation we know that some thoughtful farmers kept unpastured fields, or left uncut hay, or in the fall gathered extra fodder, all to feed visitors' horses. Apart from the religious services, the communion season was a festive time, a time of warm friendship, intimate visits, wonderful sports and games for children, courting opportunities for youth, and good meals for everyone, all blessed and sanctioned by high religious purposes.

This old pattern was inadequate to serve the number of people who flocked to Cane Ridge in 1801. Many did not want to miss any of the excitement, particularly during the nighttime, and an unprecedented number of families came prepared to camp on the grounds. On this one issue, almost alone at Cane Ridge, all witnesses offered roughly similar estimates—that approximately 140 wagons or carriages encamped on the grounds, at least for the weekend events. Apparently these campers were on their own. They found a shady spot for their wagons and slept either in the covered wagons or under attached shelters. They prepared food in the open and tethered their horses to trees much as for normal Sunday services. But it was not so simple as this description might imply. Horses had to have water twice a day, and this meant riding or leading them a goodly distance to a pond, spring, or creek. One of the mysteries of Cane Ridge is how the people attending procured the water needed even for themselves. Horses and mules also required either pasture or hay, plus the ears of corn that farmers probably brought along in the wagons. And 140 parked wagons take up a lot of space (one witness said they covered an area equal to four city blocks).

Fortunately, most families had moved west in the preceding fifteen years and had learned a great deal about camping. They knew what to bring in the way of food and supplies, what to expect, particularly if it rained (which it did on Friday, Saturday, and Sunday). Unmentioned by anyone were other logistical issues, such as toilet facilities for so many people (in his diary Lyle noted his early morning retirement into the woods). Camping details must have required much time and effort by adults, particularly the women. Although religious services of some type were continual at Cane Ridge, a fair share of the on-site campers had to be absent at any one time to tend to their chores. This need alone helps account for the constant movement of people witnessed at Cane Ridge.

As church people later used the label, Cane Ridge was not a proper camp meeting. At a poorly located site, one lacking water, the informal campers enjoyed no prior planning, adhered to no regulations, and did not have available any tents or cabins. Only one Methodist itinerant, used to camping on circuit, built a self-standing tent from poles covered with papaw leaves. Yet Cane Ridge helped stimulate planned camping. Within two years, dozens of ministers and entrepreneurs began organizing camp meetings. Within a decade practically every Methodist circuit had an annual camp, whereas the more evangelical Presbyterians soon converted their sacramental services into camp meetings.[17]

17. Lyle diary, 21–35; Redford, *History of Methodism in Kentucky*, 1:356–57.

For an unprecedentedly large number of campers (possibly 800), Cane Ridge offered a new type of experience. Camping allowed them to extend the scope, and to blur the boundaries, of distinctively religious activities. It also broadened the range of social contacts, much as group camps do today. Instead of the more familial setting of home hospitality, campers confronted something close to an urban neighborhood. They clustered, made up a crowd. And some clearly loved the experience. This deliberate clustering, often in a restricted space, became the norm for American camping, in contrast to a lonely wilderness experience. For rural Americans, going to camp literally became a way of creating temporary cities, with all the diverse people, the bustle, the excitement, and even the personal anonymity of street life. It involved people in a social environment far removed from their lonely cabins and allowed them to escape old roles and assume new ones. Add a heady dose of religious ecstasy, and people could literally lose themselves in self-justifying experiences that enabled them to forget, or temporarily transcend, the strains and problems of everyday life. Camp meetings offered escape, renewal, and recreation, all sanctioned by ostensibly religious goals. Cane Ridge initiated many people into this type of camping experience, and innovative institutions very quickly provided order and continuity for such experience. The two together constituted the camp meeting and a variety of functionally similar modern substitutes, such as summer youth camps and adult retreat centers. Remove the religious motifs, secularize the goals, and what emerges is the outlines of present-day campgrounds and resorts, not a few of which actually derived from earlier camp meetings.

The first planned religious services came on Friday evening. As host, Barton Stone undoubtedly gave an opening welcome, with a colleague, Matthew Houston, offering the scheduled sermon. Rain curtailed the numbers as yet on the grounds. The services were in a packed meetinghouse, where some lingered all night. But the real excitement was still to come. The grounds filled on Saturday. The campers, if not already in place, moved in. And thousands of people flooded in for the day from the mid-state area, including not only those who lived in horseback riding range, but uncounted hundreds who found living accommodations in neighboring communities. Single men stayed in taverns or slept on the hay in barns as far away as Lexington. People moved to and fro continually on all the roads and paths leading to Cane Ridge.

Contemporary estimates of the numbers on the grounds for Saturday and Sunday afternoon ranged up to and beyond 20,000, with the lowest but probably more reliable accounts around 10,000. The higher numbers beggar belief, not only because of the propensity of almost all observers to overestimate the number of people in any assembly but even more on logistical grounds. Most daily visitors had to come by wagon or on horses. Imagine the space needed to accommodate even up to 5,000 horses or mules. Thus, the upper range of people present at any one time could hardly have been more than 10,000. At least on Sunday afternoon, this many may have been on the grounds or in the general area. But it is quite possible that 20,000 were at Cane Ridge at some time during the next six days.

Saturday, the first great day at Cane Ridge, was supposed to be a period of preparation. Serious Christians were to ready themselves spiritually for the coming communion. Already in the participating congregations, most had joined in special prayers at society meetings, others in the traditional day of fasting. But the growing mob of people on the grounds quickly dissipated any central focus on the approaching sacrament. The Saturday morning services were reasonably quiet, like the lull before a storm. But by afternoon the preaching was continual, from both the meetinghouse and the tent. John Lyle preached from the tent, followed by the wild young Richard McNemar, who preached like a Methodist, with ecstasy and joy reflected on his face. McNemar referred to a "true new gospel," an expression that was almost unintelligible to the increasingly disillusioned Lyle. Yet it certainly inspired the crowds. The excitement built, and before dark the grounds echoed penitent cries and shouts punctuated by the crying of babies and the screaming of children and the neighing of horses. When visitors first arrived they were astonished at the sound, the sheer level of noise. James Finley, son of Cane Ridge's founding minister Robert Finley, referred to it as like the roar of Niagara. People could hear it at great distances.

Even by Saturday evening tensions rose among the ministers. None were unalterably against the exercises. But some, like Lyle, believed it wrong for the ministers deliberately to stimulate such emotional extremes. He all but despised McNemar. Stone left him more puzzled. He was not a wild preacher, in fact not as inspirational or moving as Lyle himself. But he did nothing to restrain McNemar and Houston, would not command order, and would not have those in distress or on the floor carried from the meetinghouse. Such was the widespread distress, and the confusion, that by Saturday night even McNemar was worried. Lyle, McNemar, and Houston thus decided to preach unscheduled nighttime sermons from the tent, sermons which may have focused the crowd's attention but surely did not lower the level of religious concern. With the crowd still in turmoil, the fatigued Lyle finally retired to the camp of one of his friends to gain needed sleep while others slept on the ground or in the meetinghouse.

The central purpose of the gathering—the communion—took place as scheduled in the meetinghouse on Sunday. Robert Marshall, the minister of a nearby congregation, preached the traditional action sermon outside, at the tent. But communicants moved into the meetinghouse for the serving of the elements. Responsible counts of the number of communicants ranged from 800 to 1,100 or, in one report by a Presbyterian minister, an unimaginable 7,000, with the actual number probably around 900. The tables were as usual set up in the shape of a cross in the aisles of the meetinghouse. Since it is inconceivable that more than 100 could be seated at a time, at least eight table settings succeeded one another during the long afternoon, with a huge consumption of bread and wine (another logistical detail for the local congregations). Members of at least ten Presbyterian congregations in central Kentucky actively cooperated in the communion.

Methodists were welcome, and Methodist ministers reported that many of their people came to the tables. Yet only Presbyterian ministers presided. Stone, who had contacted Methodist ministers in the planning, and who had become a friend of a leading local Methodist minister, William Burke, back in east Tennessee in 1796, clearly was more enthusiastic about ecumenical cooperation than most of his colleagues, who apparently believed that only Presbyterians should preach the institution for their own traditional communion services. Also, according to the normal pattern, Stone and his colleagues prescheduled their own ministers for set appointments in the meetinghouse or at the tent. Methodist ministers thus often felt excluded.

Given the reasonably precise estimate of communicants, one can reckon (again inexactly) the central core of participants at Cane Ridge. Probably most families who came any distance to a communion service had at least one adult who planned to take the sacrament. But children and noncommunicating adults easily exceeded the number directly involved. Thus one can estimate that at least 2,000, and possibly more, seriously involved Presbyterians were at Cane Ridge on Sunday, a core group only marginally larger than at many other such communions. Because of Stone's openness, his special invitation, and the expected magnitude of the occasion, more Methodists than usual attended, but it is inconceivable that more than 200 took communion.

Firsthand reports identify thirteen Presbyterian ministers who either preached or served tables at Cane Ridge. In retrospect, Stone and others noted eighteen Presbyterian ministers present, a number that corresponds nicely with the number of local ministers who were almost certainly present because of the proximity of their congregations. A few participating ministers came from a great distance—two from Ohio and one from near the Tennessee border in Logan County. At least four identified Methodist ministers preached. This number excludes a potentially larger number of lay exhorters who were on the grounds. At least one unidentified black minister, probably but not conclusively Old Captain, the founder and longtime minister of the first African Baptist Church in Lexington, preached to a separate Negro assembly.[18] References to numerous Baptists on the grounds, and to the attendance of white Baptist preachers, suggest that some of them exhorted, but none are recorded as preaching in the church or from the tent. In a sacrament on the next weekend at Paint Creek, two Baptists preached from the tent, but since the Baptists would not take communion with improperly baptized Christians, they must have felt a bit alien. Although only ministers preached prepared sermons, or had allocated times to perform, literally hundreds of people served as exhorters at Cane Ridge. In the tumult the distinction between prepared sermons (with a theme or text taken from the Bible and carefully developed points or arguments) and more spontaneous exhortations (extemporaneous or even impromptu practical advice, or tearful appeals or warnings) dissolved, particularly when outlying members of the audience could not even hear the sermons.

Given a core audience of only 2,500 or so, how can one account for the soaring estimates of people present at Cane Ridge? A crowd of 2,500 serious Christians was itself hardly a small gathering in rural Kentucky in 1801, but these people clearly made up a minority of those present, particularly on Sunday. Descriptions of what happened on Saturday spread with every horseback rider who left the grounds. By Sunday it seems that everyone in accessible range wanted to see what

18. Bishop, ed., *An Outline of the History of the Church*, 230–34.

was going on. One suspects that practically everyone with an opportunity managed to get to Cane Ridge, from the governor of the state on down to farm laborers and slaves. It was a circus, the most exciting event in years. Why would anyone who could possibly get there miss something like this on a balmy, humid summer weekend, with the crops all laid by? Thus, as at Cambuslang in 1742, the majority of people at Cane Ridge were casual visitors or outsiders, some only curious spectators. This does not mean that all but a very small minority were unresponsive to the religious content of the services or openly mocked or ridiculed what happened. Most, churched or unchurched, held basic Christian beliefs. They came not only to observe and to join in the excitement, but also to listen to able ministers, even though they had no desire to take communion. Finally—and this is the most intriguing but elusive motive—several must have come with some feeling of guilt, some trembling anticipation that they might join in the extreme physical exercises, which both drew and repelled so many spectators.

Apparently the wildest exercises remained outside the meetinghouse. The communion service seemed orderly. For some it had a deep religious meaning. Lyle wrote that he had "clearer views of divine things than . . . before" as he took communion, and felt "uncommonly tender" as he spoke at his serving of the tables. Two neighboring ministers, not usually given to wild emotionalism, wept at the tables.

Outside, the groaning and falling continued. Some people experienced only weakened knees or a light head (including Governor James Garrard from nearby Paris, who was a former Baptist minister but was then considered by the Baptists an apostate unitarian). Others fell but remained conscious or talkative; a few fell into a deep coma, with the symptoms of a grand mal seizure or a type of hysteria. Crowds gathered around each person who swooned. Estimates of the number slain rose by Tuesday to 3,000, surely an exaggeration (more modest estimates ranged from 300 to 1,000). Perhaps for the first time in American religious history, falling to the ground became almost the norm, in no wise exceptional. Some parts of the grounds were literally strewn like a battlefield.

Observers confessed their inability to describe the scene. Language, they said, could not do it justice. Yet no present historian can improve upon the following report by Colonel Patterson. Imagine a large congregation, Patterson wrote,

> assembled in the woods, ministers preaching day and night; the camp illuminated with candles, on trees, at waggons, and at the tent; persons falling down, and carried out of the crowd, by those next to them, and taken to some convenient place, where prayer is made for them; some Psalm or Hymn suitable to the occasion, sung. If they speak, what they say is attended to, being very solemn and affecting—many are struck under such exhortations. But if they do not recover soon, praying and singing is kept up, alternatively, and sometimes a minister exhorts over them—for generally a large group of people collect, and stand around, paying attention to prayer and joining in singing. Now suppose 20 of these groups around; a minister engaged in preaching to a large congregation, in the middle, some mourning, some rejoicing, and great solemnity on every countenance, and you will form some imperfect idea of the extraordinary work![19]

A minister, probably James Campbell, noted that some of the people who were down eventually felt comfort, or in their terms "got through;" others never did. Those who succeeded often arose with shouts of joy, and then began their own exhortations. The minister described the awesome scene:

> Sinners dropping down on every hand, shrieking, groaning, crying for mercy, convoluted; professors [of religion] praying, agonizing, fainting, falling down in distress, for sinners, or in raptures of joy! Some singing, some shouting, clapping their hands,

19. Paterson to King, September 25, 1801, in *Increase of Piety,* 39–40. No readers, at least among Presbyterians and Methodists, could have missed this letter.

hugging and even kissing, laughing; others talking to the distressed, to one another, or to opposers of the work, and all this at once—no spectacle can excite a stronger sensation. And with what is doing, the darkness of the night, the solemnity of the place, and of the occasion, and conscious guilt, all conspire to make terror thrill through every power of the soul, and rouse it to awful attention.[20]

Soon the sheer confusion practically subverted the outdoor preaching. Small groups joined in prayer or in loud hymn singing, with singing the most enjoyable group activity and the one that often most affected an audience. Almost as prominent as falling were various bodily movements. Convulsive motions dated at least from early Scottish communions, and after Cane Ridge would become known, collectively and misleadingly, as the "jerks." The term concealed the diversity of such motion, including rhythmic dancing. More conventional shouts and groans joined with a near babble of speech, some incoherent, some later distinguished as holy laughter or singing. The endless activity never quite ceased, even in the early morning hours. Some people stayed up all night. People who chose to stay on the grounds grabbed moments of sleep wherever they could, including some in the meetinghouse. Fatigued ministers were continually in demand to attend the slain, to pray with the penitent, and to calm the hysterical.

But most impressive of all to many spectators were the exhortations. Here and there almost anyone, including those who rose from the ground as well as child converts, might burst out with an exhortation. Women, small children, slaves, shy people, illiterate people, all exhorted with great effect. Observers marveled at their eloquence, their deep feeling, and often their seeming preternatural understanding of scripture. Some believed the newly converted enjoyed the gift of prophecy, while critics often believed them possessed by demons.

20. Letter from a Kentucky minister included in a letter from Moses Hoge to Dr. Ashbel Green, September 10, 1801, in *Increase of Piety,* 53.

One perceptive observer, who arrived at Cane Ridge on Saturday, when the "work" was already in full swing, estimated that 300 people exhorted, many at the same time. He was particularly taken by a seven-year-old girl who mounted a man's shoulders (typical for children) and spoke wondrous words until she was completely fatigued. When she lay her head on his as if to sleep, a person in the audience suggested that the poor thing had better be laid down, presumably to sleep. The girl roused at this suggestion and said, "Don't call me poor, for Christ is my brother, God my father, and I have a kingdom to inherit, and therefore do not call me poor, for I am rich in the blood of the Lamb." The theological images are confused, the words quite compatible with those of a child who had learned religious language from her parents, but nonetheless such words from the mouth of a babe seemed almost unbelievable to those who crowded around.[21]

Escape was as easy as walking away. Some came as others left. Arrivals provided fuel for the revival fires, even as exhausted converts left rejoicing for their homes. No one could tally the results. Saints and sinners alike experienced the despair or the ecstasy. Some believed themselves converted. Some gained what they called "comfort," or a secure sense that they had received God's grace. Other ostensibly pious Christians often became insecure about their own salvation because of the explosive experience of children or neighbors ("It never happened that way to me"). No one knows how many experienced conversion. Stone later estimated that between 500 and 1,000 were converted, but the very range of his estimate made clear the impossibility of any accurate count. In fact, in all the confusion, even ministers lost all clear guidelines as to what marked conversion.

The peak day was Sunday. As faithful Presbyterians submitted their leaden tokens and joined in what had to have been a

---

21. Letter from a gentleman to his sister in Philadelphia, August 10, 1801, in *Gospel News*, 45. The same incident is reported in a letter from a Presbyterian minister in Kentucky to another in Philadelphia, August 1801, in *Methodist Magazine* 25 (1802): 264.

distracted communion, and as other Presbyterian ministers gave their scheduled sermons from the tent, some Methodists felt excluded. William Burke, one of Methodism's most powerful and esteemed preachers, resented his exclusion from the administration of the communion and access to the tent. He therefore moved to a fallen tree that was fifteen feet above the ground and a hundred feet east of the meetinghouse and made this his pulpit. His opening prayers and hymns gained him a huge audience (he estimated 10,000, an incredible number), perhaps because so many of the spectators were not able to gain access to either the meetinghouse or the area before the tent. When Lyle came by, he found Burke's audience in an ecstasy of singing and hand-shaking. Burke's new pulpit became the most tumultuous of four centers of activity, including also the tent, the meetinghouse, and a Negro assembly area, probably about 150 yards southeast of the church. Dozens of informal circles or organized or semi-organized prayer groups met at the various camping sites, most of which must have been on or near the ridge to the northwest of the meetinghouse.

By Monday, many visitors had to leave. But the momentum of the revival was such that no one could terminate it. New arrivals kept coming until Wednesday or even, by some reports, Thursday, when organized activity finally dribbled to a stop. Ministers who went home with their flocks often felt a moral obligation to come back to minister to all the people in distress. Some ministers coming from great distances apparently did not arrive until Sunday or Monday. Such was the immediate reputation of Cane Ridge that people who at first missed it now wanted to be part of it. Even ministers such as the diarist John Lyle, who was leery of so much that happened and repulsed by the role of several fellow ministers, felt that, in the midst of all the chaos, the revival somehow continued. Some people, including precious youth, were gloriously affected. Lyle rejoiced in such returns and did not want to block the revival, even as he feared excesses would soon doom it.

After the thanksgiving sermons on Monday, the normal communion schedule had been fulfilled. What followed was seren-
dipitous, guided by the Spirit or by the multitudes, who continued to demand more singing, praying, and preaching. In
this, Cane Ridge presaged later, protracted revivals that began
without any set termination date.[22]

That is it—the Cane Ridge story. It quickly became one of
the best-reported events in American history. Only John Lyle
had kept a diary of events as they happened, but at least a
dozen participants wrote letters to religious publications or to
distant friends. As the years passed, others wrote memoirs of
the event. A few of the Methodist ministers, such as Burke,
who were so involved in the revival that they decided not to
join Asbury at the district conference in east Tennessee, soon
offered their critique. Of course, they gave a Methodist flavor
to the revival, claiming a priority or a special effectiveness that

22. The above account of Cane Ridge is based largely on contemporary witnesses, although my visit to the Cane Ridge site informed some of my more tentative attempts to
describe the physical setting. Most of the letters about Cane Ridge appeared in more than one
evangelical magazine, often with minor differences in text or longer or shorter versions of
handwritten originals, none of which are now available. These textual problems do not challenge the overall narrative as I have presented it, but they do make it difficult to cite references. What follows are the main sources, but without duplicate citations.

Least reliable are the memories of Cane Ridge written by participants many years later.
These include Barton W. Stone's autobiography, *A Short History of the Life of Barton W. Stone,*
chaps. 5 and 6, and his "History of the Christian Church," chap. 1, in *The Christian Messenger,*
February 24, 1827; Richard M'Nemar, *The Kentucky Revival* (1808); David Purviance, *The
Biography of Elder David Purviance, Written by Himself* (Dayton: n.p., 1848); James B. Finley,
Autobiography (Cincinnati: Methodist Book Concern, 1867); William Burke, *Autobiography,*
in James B. Finley, *Sketches of Western Methodism* (Cincinnati: Methodist Book Concern,
1855); Theophilus Arminius, "Account of the Rise and Progress of the Work of God in the
Western Country," *Methodist Magazine* 2 (May 1819): 184–87.

Three critical evaluations of Cane Ridge, and of the revivals for which it was a prototype,
were written so close to the event as to constitute sources: Adam Rankin, *A Review of the
Noted Revival in Kentucky* (Lexington, Ky.: Bradford, 1802); David Rice, *Sermon on the Present
Revival of Religion* (Lexington, Ky.: Chapless, 1803); John Cree et al. [spokesmen for the
Associate Synod, or the old Scottish Seceders], *Evils of the Work Now Prevailing in the United
States of America, Under the Name of a Revival of Religion* (Washington: n.p., 1804).

The most detailed source of all is the diary of John Lyle (esp. pp. 21–35), which survives as
a very legible manuscript at the Kentucky Historical Society, and is also available there on
microfilm. Several inexact typescripts of this invaluable diary are available at, for example,
the University of Chicago and the University of Kentucky. It is clear that Lyle actually wrote
some of his notes well after the events he described, and thus with the advantage of hindsight.

events did not quite justify. Unfortunately, all the firsthand reports were by men, all by whites, and apparently none by anyone deeply affected by the exercises. These witnesses leave us many puzzles. Some deserve extended analysis.

One puzzle, largely unanswerable, is how ordinary lay people experienced Cane Ridge. We have no questionnaires, no post-revival interviews. Lyle tried to gather as many impressions as possible, but these soon became almost stereotypical. Obviously, what people expected and what religious understanding they had influenced their reactions. Since almost everyone in the area seemed to have attended, the revival reflected the religious diversity of central Kentucky. Some devout Presbyterians and Methodists reflected a high level of doctrinal understanding, while other nominal Christians, with limited experience in churches, must have had little doctrinal sophistication. Critics ranged from professed Christians who rejected an evangelical or crisis-conversion approach to salvation to avowed rationalists or deists and, possi-

---

Much less detailed is Robert Patterson's "An Account of the Revival of Religion," which is published in part in Catharine C. Cleveland, *The Great Revival in the West, 1797–1805* (Chicago: University of Chicago Press, 1916), app. 7, pp. 196–201.

The letters, with only one or two exceptions, appeared in multiple evangelical publications. I here cite only one reference for each: letter from a Presbyterian in Bourbon County to a friend in Baltimore, August 7, 1801; from a gentleman to his sister in Philadelphia, August 10, 1801; Dr. Rev. Rogers to his publisher, November 2, 1801, in *Gospel News*, 4–5, 7. Colonel James Paterson to Rev. John King, September 25, 1801, with comments by King; George Baxter to Archibald Alexander, January 1, 1802, *New York Missionary Magazine and Repository of Religious Intelligence*, 3 (1902): 118–26, 86–92. Moses Hoge to Ashbel Green, September 10, 1801, with excerpts from a letter from a minister from Kentucky recounting the recent revivals; from a gentleman in Lancaster to his friend in Philadelphia, February 2, 1801, containing a letter from a gentlemen in Kentucky to his brother; James Finley to his uncle, September 20, 1801; excerpt from a religious journal in Lancaster containing a letter from John Evans Findley to W. J. R. Dickson, with Finley's accounts of Cane Ridge; from a gentleman in Washington, Kentucky, to his son in Philadelphia, February 26, July 15, 1801; from Rev. John Smith, Northwest Territory, September 7, 1801, in *Increase of Piety*, 52–54, 80–81, 85–91, 93–96, 101. Letter from F. Hughes, after a visit to Rev. James Welch in Lexington, Kentucky, November 23, 1801; from James Welch, Lexington, to editors, July 15, 1802, *Connecticut Evangelical Magazine* 2 (April 1802): 393–94; 3 (September 1802): 19–20. Letter from a Presbyterian minister in Kentucky to another in Philadelphia, August 1801; from John Evans Findley of Mason County, Kentucky, n.d. (this is slightly different from the above letter by Findley), *Methodist Magazine* 25 (1802): 264; 26 (1803): 125–27.

bly, a few atheists. Even among evangelicals, the doctrinal distance between Calvinists and Arminians should have produced a quite different understanding of the salvation drama enacted on the grounds. But one cannot assume any deep or profound doctrinal sophistication for most of the lay audience, and experiences were therefore probably more congruent than doctrines would suggest. Such was the generalized Protestant Christian culture of the area that most people, even casual spectators, had some comprehension of what the preachers emphasized—what salvation entailed, what sinfulness meant, what immortality promised, and what a rebirth experience required. The ministers referred to deists and atheists who, surprisingly often, fell with other sinners. What is not clear is how they defined the terms, or how such labels really fit what must have been a small minority of spectators.

Whatever the intellectual resources of those affected at Cane Ridge (and most people seemed affected to some degree), the context did not invite any profound understanding. Such was the noise and disorder that few had much opportunity to hear any extended sermons, let alone probe deeply into doctrinal issues. They had to make do with their own developed resources or, as so many did, petition their pastors or trusted friends to give them a better understanding. The near anarchy meant that people confronted something very primordial, primitive, or visceral, with an intensity that momentarily overwhelmed any desire for self-conscious conceptualization. Thus, people with no religious training or confessional tradition were as vulnerable to the exercises as anyone else but were then ill-equipped to make sense of it all. Even the frequent breakdown of normal language—the laughter, the babble of unintelligible speech—suggested the primal nature of the experience.

From all that we know about popular Christianity, even from the detailed phenomenological evidence collected at Cambuslang, we can assume that Satan, or the Devil, held a very prominent place in the popular understanding of what happened at Cane Ridge. Proper doctrinal refinements have rarely controlled popular beliefs about a spirit world, a world of incorporeal beings, from angels and demons to the "haunts" or ghosts that hovered in the background of every village. For scriptural reasons, any version of Christian doctrine must account for spirits, beings whose status is between that of humans and gods. But in all forms of Christian orthodoxy, spirits are created by God, fully dependent upon his will for their being and behavior, and subject to his ultimate judgment and to whatever fate he had decreed for them. Angels denote not only specific, semidivine, named persons noted in the scriptures, but choirs of such obedient spirits. Demons or devils denote rebellious spirits, lending to the spirit world the same disjunctive divisions as characterize the human—saints and sinners. Satan, by orthodox understanding, is the chief among rebellious spirits, the counterpart of Adam, one who originally rebelled against God and, at least so long as God permits, tries to recruit other angels and human beings for his rebellion. This is about as far as one can generalize about Satan, for at least in the Western church Satan has rarely become an object of careful doctrinal explication, let alone theological refinement. Individual Christians have as a consequence had plenty of leeway for imaginative embellishment, and the record, including that on witchcraft, suggests that they have always been quite inventive in filling in all the hidden dimensions of the kingdom of darkness.

Irrepressible in popular Christianity has been the dominant heresy of the church—ontological dualism. Manichaeism has lived on. The forces of good and evil battle through the ages, and human beings still feel that they are enlisting in the ranks of one or the other. Not that any would-be Christians ever viewed Satan as the full equal of Jehovah. From the scriptures they knew that, sooner or later, Jehovah would win out in the struggle and then chain and neutralize Satan. But even this unequal struggle, as people so easily understood it, still involved two autonomous individuals, or really two deities.

People did not, and often for compelling reasons did not want to, view Satan as a creature of God, unchained by God, fully under God's providence, even doing God's will, and in some sense necessarily contributing to God's glory. This, like God as the source of evil, seemed inconsistent with the image of the God they loved. At the popular level, as William James persuasively argued, almost no one ever really believed in divine omnipotence. Such a belief was intellectually inconceivable and morally repugnant. Popular Christianity was, in practice but not in confession, ontologically pluralistic. Jehovah was in some sense limited or finite. Satan and angels and people were not completely under his control. Their relationahip to God, although not one of equality, was still dialogistic, a matter of negotiation, even when God had all the good cards. It is quite probable that the less theologically sophisticated people at Cane Ridge believed that they had attended an unusually dramatic confrontation between God and Satan, and that they understood their own drama of salvation as a microcosm of this vast cosmic struggle. They quite literally battled to escape Satan. Even the language of ministers fostered such a completely heretical understanding.

For good reason, all the prerational experiences at Cane Ridge and the oversimplified theological understanding frightened some of the Presbyterian clergy. They represented a venerable religious tradition, one tied to systematic doctrines. It was a tradition that justified, even exalted, deep feelings or a type of experiential religion, but always in the context of proper understanding. The complementary poles of experience and reason broke apart at Cane Ridge. At best, the doctrinal component lost precision and distinctiveness and lapsed into a vague, general, loose, sentimental, or even visceral version of Christianity. Even the ecumenical flavor—Cane Ridge was a meeting ground for doctrinal diversity—threatened the Presbyterian tradition. So many present did not properly understand the traditional sacramental service. Most did not even come to participate. They did not care about such established forms. The old religion required learning, the assimilation of beliefs and attitudes, and a relatively homogeneous religious community. In the American West, for the first time, Scotch-Irish Presbyterians were losing such homogeneity. They mixed and mingled with all the other people in the area. Even compact ethnic communities quickly broke down, as Baptist, Presbyterian, and Methodist families all took up land in a noncontiguous fashion. The church still provided a type of ethnic-religious isolation for people with common traditions, but even these began to erode at Cane Ridge. There the promiscuous mixing threatened all confessional-liturgical traditions. It eroded away the advantages of Presbyterians in the West, gave the Methodists a competitive edge, and promised a continued degeneration of the more demanding and rigorous forms of Calvinist piety. The more conservative Presbyterian ministers thus had compelling reasons to be apprehensive.

But even as conservatives had forebodings of future disaster, at least a few Presbyterian ministers rejoiced in what happened at Cane Ridge. First among these was Barton Stone, the host minister, who had never quite grasped or embraced the more subtle tenets of Calvinism, and who already craved the unity of all Christians. Equally pleased were the "hot" ministers, those who shared with Methodists a craving for a highly experiential or spiritual religion, one that could bring people close to ecstasy almost daily. Rather than trying to order the chaos at Cane Ridge, they enjoyed it. They helped create it and communicated a clear message to those present—go with the Spirit. Rejoice! Two Presbyterians who fit this pattern were Richared McNemar and John Rankin. Notably, both would soon convert to America's first Pentecostal sect, the Shakers.

The greatest puzzles all relate to the physical exercises. Cane Ridge gained its greatest fame for the extent of these exercises. Much later, Stone offered his own misleading taxonomy. The legendary Methodist circuit minister, Peter Cartwright, a youth of sixteen at the time of the Cane Ridge communion and a convert at the same Logan County sacrament that Stone had visited in May 1801, further caricatured these exercises as an old man, particularly by his wild stories about the jerks. Early twentieth-century historians of evangelical religion, such as Sweet and Cleveland, looking back from an uncomprehending age, either offered simplified psychological explanations of such "perversions" or explained them by the terror or barbarism of the frontier. The wild exercises have therefore continued to amaze and titillate modern audiences. This failure to understand the exercises has almost forced historians to see them as frontier aberrations, or as irrational "diseases" that infected psychologically sick members of the lower orders of society—poor, ignorant, and superstitious.

No magical insights can replace these historical myths. But some corrective facts are quite clear. The physical exercises at Cane Ridge, as at a hundred other revivals early in the nineteenth century, did not correlate with social class. At Cane Ridge many leading citizens were deeply affected, beginning with the governor. A local farmer and able county representative to the Kentucky Assembly, David Purviance, was so affected at Cane Ridge as to give up politics and become a minister. Other prominent landowners, the gentry of the area, were also affected. Lyle's diary reveals that the people most stricken were often sturdy landowners or prominent women, leaders in the local congregations, people in the upper ranks of early Kentucky society. Descriptions of the exercises among participants in the subsequent North Carolina revivals move easily from illiterate blacks to country squires, from self-proclaimed deists to pious Christians. A few Presbyterian ministers, despite their college degrees, experienced convulsions or fell into comas, although they rarely did so within the pulpit. The exercises at times seemed to affect women and children disproportionately, but not always. At least two-thirds of those Lyle reported as down at Cane Ridge were women or girls, but this estimate may accurately represent only their numbers within the churches. Clearly, young people were disproportionately among those who believed themselves converted, but this circumstance stemmed from the fact that they were the largest component of people outside the church. One contextual factor—the number of people who went without food for a day or longer in the midst of heat and humidity—may have increased slightly the number who felt light-headed or even those who fainted. But this explanation is at best marginal, since the same exercises continued at subsequent communions where provisions were plentiful and the weather cool.

Another needed correction is to point out that these physical exercises were not new or unprecedented, not nearly so distinctive as so many of the amazed observers assumed. In the total perspective of Christianity, they were relatively mild and quite innocuous in their consequences. They bear no comparison with the hysterical manias, massive pilgrimages, and self-flagellations that infrequently punctuated medieval Catholicism, let alone the wildest excesses of what Christians deemed pagan religions. They do bear comparison to the ring shouts and dancing so often observed in black religious services, which were probably a survival of African religious practices. Indeed, black religion in the South may have had some influence on expected or sanctioned ways of giving bent to religious ecstasy at Cane Ridge. What the exercises revealed were religiously serious people who, in a powerfully suggestive environment, chose, or were forced, to reenact the drama of Jesus' passion and the ever-recurring drama of their own tortured quest for salvation. These mutually reinforcing dramas forced people toward experiential poles—on one hand the extreme of personal revulsion and self-doubt, on the other that of exaltation and joy.

The communion service had proven, for over two hundred years of Presbyterian history, the perfect vehicle for making these dramas vivid and personally relevant. The Scottish communion normally, for almost all who fully participated, led to intense experiences, to cathartic tears and to rare, liberating, redemptive moments, so precious that, for some people, they justified life itself. The Catholic Mass served the same purpose for the truly devout. The faithful might consequently come to the familiar and suggestive judgment that a nontearful religion was no religion at all. Tears, either of remorse or of joy, are at the heart of any affectional religion. Beyond tears are the more extreme but equally involuntary effects—verbal or muscular or neurological. These, too, are within the range of almost everyone's experience, as in rare and often unwanted moments of overwhelming feeling, such as at the death of a loved one. Who can then resist tears? Or cries of despair? Or even the writhing and convulsive movements that may provide an outlet for complete personal desolation? Surely no one expects a quiet demeanor or reasonable rationalization at such moments. Nor for those often unsought, often inexplicable moments of sheer exaltation which, for some people, may be approached in a sexual orgasm. In other words, some form of physical expression fitted these occasions, whether in an avowedly religious or a secular setting. Physical effects are not in themselves different whatever the stimulant. After all, some people largely identify swooning with rock concerts or find in Woodstock the clearest parallel to Cane Ridge.

The "physical exercises" at Cane Ridge were appropriately named. They were indeed physical. And they involved extreme, extended muscular movements. No aerobic exercise could match some of the jerking and dancing, and those most exercised reported extreme muscular soreness as one result. Those affected, some at the cost of great embarrassment, invariably agreed that what they did was involuntary. They could not help it. A few undoubtedly faked it, choosing to join in the deliberate abandonment and merely imitating what others did. But for most, these movements were beyond any self-control, even in cases when people deliberately tried to resist shouts or rhythmic movements. Scarcely anyone present seemed immune to some physical effects. All that was required was that one be in some sense sensitive to the feelings and moods of other people. It was as if a miasma hung over Cane Ridge, to ensnare anyone who came within its range. For the pious, this miasma was the Holy Spirit. They had ready conceptual tools to account for what happened. It made sense to them. But such an understanding was not necessary in order to have the experience, just as some people read into the exercises quite different meanings. The interpretation, in other words, did not seem to control what happened to people. The situation was comparable to that of a person who stumbles into a funeral, one governed by unappreciated or even incomprehensible ethnic conventions, yet who soon succumbs to the intense emotion and joins the group in uncontrollable weeping and moaning, as if by a type of identification that is more visceral than self-conscious.

Yet—and this is a critical *yet* —the physical exercises at Cane Ridge were culturally conditioned. To some extent they were learned, even when they seemed completely involuntary. To some extent they were contrived, both by those who exhorted and by those who listened and responded. Certain techniques, which ministers conscientiously learned, helped push audiences toward an ecstatic frenzy. Certain hymns, certain tunes worked better than others. Certain repeated and familiar verbal images, those with great resonance for an audience, worked better than others. In many of the greatest revivals the spark was a type of confession—the telling of what had happened to oneself there or at an earlier revival. Some ministers learned the most evocative ways of telling their stories. Several sermonic devices—timing, phrasing, pauses, and above all the display of intense feeling— worked. On the other hand, disapproving ministers could at least moderate, if not prevent, such exercises.

It did not take long for certain exercises to become rituals, familiar, expected, and either sanctioned or tolerated. The outlet for intense feeling soon came to have a conventional form, one that was learned, and thus one conditioned by role models. But all of this does not contradict the testimony of individuals who reported later that they could not help shouting in the middle of a sermon, or falling to the floor during communion, or jerking spasmodically or rhythmically during hymn singing. Had they been elsewhere, members of a different religion, in the midst of a different crowd, their physical exercises would have taken quite different forms, yet their actions would have been just as involuntary.

The repertoire of physical options, however extreme or bizarre, still had limits. In any religious context, in any moment of intense feeling, the physical manifestations always involve various movements and sounds. (For Richard McNemar they also involved heavenly fragrances.) And in any such context, the body may eventually reach a state of neurological overload. The one commonality across cultural boundaries is this limit condition—fainting. From weak knees to a deep coma, physiology can overpower culture. At various points people make choices, but at this limit point they move beyond any choice. It is notable that almost all witnesses at Cane Ridge, or outsiders who rushed to Kentucky to observe subsequent sacraments, took the falling as the new and alarming phenomenon that most cried out for understanding. In the religious press, Cane Ridge quickly symbolized the falling exercise, not the trembling or jerking or crying or laughing. From the reports, it is not even clear that many people at Cane Ridge jerked, at least in the form later described by Cartwright and Stone. But that hundreds fell to the ground was beyond dispute; falling was the central phenomenon of Cane Ridge.

None of the accounts of Cane Ridge had quite the effect, or the widespread circulation, of McGready's narrative of events in Logan County. The Patterson letter was most widely circulated, occasioning a published debate and an editorial in the *New York Missionary Magazine*. What soon became, in evangelical circles, the most authoritative evaluation of the great revival in Kentucky was an extended letter from George Baxter. A prominent Presbyterian minister and educator in the Shenandoah Valley of Virginia, a participant in and warm supporter of the revival of 1787–90, and in 1801 president of Washington Academy (today Washington and Lee), Baxter came to Kentucky after Cane Ridge to observe and to report to eastern Presbyterians on the phenomenon. He sent his letter to Archibald Alexander, head of Washington's sister college Hampden-Sydney, with the clear intent that it be widely circulated. We know of at least one instance of a minister reading it to his congregation, with wondrous effect. Baxter came to Kentucky in the early fall, attended and preached at three sacraments, and personally observed all the exercises reported at Cane Ridge. Given his own affectionate preaching and his yearning for a revival, he came not to debunk but to see if the evidence pointed to an authentic work of the Spirit.

This was the big question among evangelical Christians everywhere, and one so serious as to justify Baxter's trip and investigation. Skeptics, particularly those at a distance, had profound doubts. They easily attributed the exercises to a type of popular delusion, perhaps triggered by the overly affectionate or frightening preaching of irresponsible ministers. Locally, the cantankerous old Adam Rankin wrote a book to prove that the situation was much worse, that those most exercised were literally possessed by evil spirits, and that the so-called revival, among those who had departed from scriptural worship by the introduction of human-created hymns, was a work of Satan, who above all used sensuous hymns and wild singing to capture the unwary.[23]

Baxter tried to calm eastern fears. He first noted the singularity of the sacraments. More people came than ever before. The gatherings continued longer than the normal four or five days, some lasting as long as a week. People came from up to 200 miles away, and many camped, out of necessity as well as a desire to participate fully in all the services. The size required multiple preaching stands and led to much wandering to and fro. Some confusion and disorder was inevitable. But most

23. Rankin, *Review of the Noted Revival in Kentucky*, 47–63.

distinctive of all was the large numbers who fell. Baxter, almost alone among witnesses, knew that such falling was not unique to Kentucky; he had observed a few cases in earlier revivals, knew about it in the revivals of 1740, and had read about such cases in Scotland and Ulster. He used this historical perspective to disarm critics. He also discounted the effects of falling. After the first episodes, it did not disturb worship. Those nearby quietly cared for those who had fallen. He also argued that, after dealing with the almost unmanageable crowds at Cane Ridge, the churches deliberately scheduled simultaneous communion seasons in two neighboring congregations in order to reduce the numbers. He attributed the falling to the deep conviction of sin induced by the context, and emphasized that the pious who fell were not really afflicted, but had something approximating the death experience of the very devout; they literally glimpsed God and heaven, and then gave very balanced and rational reports. In sum, such unusual and abnormal exercises were peculiarly adapted to the West, which was so full of infidelity, and they were perhaps necessary just to get the attention of a preoccupied and giddy people. He believed, incorrectly, that the early opposition was receding even by the fall of 1801. Things were under control.[24] In a follow-up letter he wisely noted the difficulties of disciplining a revival among such disparate people, immigrants from different countries, with different habits, and with many ignorant of the first principles of religion. For him, it was the cultural pluralism of the West, not the frontier, that made these revivals seem so different from those in the East.[25]

Some of the most detailed ministerial evaluations of such revivals came later. In December 1801, David Caldwell issued a call for a special New Year's communion service in Randolph County, North Carolina. This communion followed several summer sacraments in North and South Carolina that almost

24. Baxter to Alexander, January 1, 1802.
25. George Baxter, "Revival of Religion in the Western Country," *Western Missionary Magazine* 1 (January 1804): 467.

matched those in central Kentucky. Caldwell, in a sense the grandfather of the western revivals (since his students led them), was apprehensive about the extreme physical effects and wanted to meet with fellow ministers in western Carolina to discuss what had happened. He and his colleagues wanted their own revival. They did not want to miss what might be the golden moment. They hoped especially to reach their youth. Four scattered, isolated ministers in the western counties of North Carolina gathered their flocks (over a hundred in all) and made long journeys to this union meeting in the middle of winter. Some had to camp en route and experienced a wondrous work of the Spirit around their campfires.[26]

Among these ministers was Samuel E. McCorkle. Much like Caldwell, he was apprehensive about emotionalism and discounted the religious significance of the more violent exercises. He came to view the events in Randolph County, and he brought the youth of his congregation in hopes of a good effect on them. Before the meeting ended, his own son was struck down. McCorkle was eventually persuaded that the Spirit found outlet in such extreme exercises. He discovered what became a truism—it was much easier to be skeptical at a good distance. But he did not believe the extreme physical effects were more than incidental to what happened.

Here, and in subsequent union meetings (or camp meetings as they would be called by 1802), McCorkle carefully observed people, and in letters wrote down his revealing evaluations. At meeting after meeting, McCorkle toured the grounds, describing all manner of people, including as many blacks as whites (they were much more numerous in North Carolina than in Kentucky and had a much larger role in the revivals). He noted nothing exceptional in the behavior of blacks. Fainting, as at Cane Ridge, was the one common and most extreme exercise.

26. A letter from the Rev. James Hall, Iredell County, North Carolina, May 4, 1802, in William Henry Foote, *Sketches of North Carolina* (New York: Carter, 1846), 382–90, which was widely printed in evangelical journals. For these North Carolina revivals see John Boles, *The Great Revival, 1787–1805* (Lexington: University Press of Kentucky, 1972), 70–89.

From multiple observations, McCorkle made the following generalizations: that educated people, or those moral in deportment, struggled longer in their convictions, but were more regular in exercises and more fluent in talking about them. The ignorant and immoral had shorter and often more extreme exercises, but had a poor understanding of what happened. Very young and very bashful persons prayed and exhorted with facility at the moment, but later reverted to their normal diffidence. Even when exercised, their descriptions of their religious experience never went beyond the level of their education and ability (no miracles here). McCorkle decided it was better to leave undisturbed those crying for mercy, unless they asked for help or verged on complete despair. In time, many gained consolation, but McCorkle cautioned against accepting this as a mark of conversion. He awaited the moral fruits. One seven-year-old girl, under deep conviction, exhorted wonderfully, but on examination McCorkle found her deficient in understanding the Shorter Catechism. He denied her communion, then almost regretted his own tough decision. He believed it irresponsible for ministers to use prayer or exhortation to incite such exercises, because they were incidental to religious life, and he urged parents not to push children forward after their first exercise.[27]

Almost all Presbyterian ministers agreed with both Baxter and McCorkle that they had to be very cautious in interpreting the meaning of physical exercises. Sinners and saints were both susceptible. One pattern, even almost a rule, was that early in the exercises almost everyone revealed an overwhelming sense of sinfulness, and thus in various ways cried out for mercy or help. Even long-term, devout church members did this; such remorse was therefore not necessarily an indicator of the rebirth experience. For such people, ministers offered reassurance, emphasizing that conversion did not require unusual exercises. For innocent, unconverted youth, the exer-

27. Letters by Samuel M'Corkle, December 16, 1801; January 8, February 4, March 17, April 2, 1802, in Foote, *Sketches of North Carolina*, 391–99.

cises often did mark their passage into the church, although there seemed no good reason why, except the occasion and the expectation of others, that the passage had to be so rough. Ministers tried, over and over again, to make clear that extreme physical effects were unnecessary for salvation; they were not themselves a cause of salvation, but only incidental outgrowths of the normal excitement of a great revival—contextually appropriate but never normative. For adults long outside the church—those rationalists, deists, or libertines whom ministers liked to cite to prove the revival a work of the Spirit—the intense, often extended period of acute distress led, sooner or later, to at least temporary relief or a feeling of comfort. Afflicted persons interpreted this state as conversion, but ministers noted that people often quickly lost this confidence, and thus typically had to go through three or four such agonizing experiences before gaining an enduring sense of comfort. Even the emotional intensity of a Cane Ridge could not hasten the work of the Spirit. For uncomprehending spectators, for blatantly immoral people who sometimes jerked or fainted, the emotional experience did not seem to have any necessary, or enduring, religious meaning at all, even when such people in the midst of the exercises used conventional religious language to characterize their distress. A cautious minister always awaited moral proof before admitting new communicants.

At times, and at certain points of developed anticipation, ministers had little direct control over the revivals. The physical effects spread beyond the communion services, the societies, or Sunday worship. At times of great religious excitement, people swooned at home or in the fields. Men behind the plow got the jerks. Under conviction, housewives agonized for days. Clearly for some it was the drama of salvation, not the influence of crowds, that elicited the exercises. But even such isolated individuals reflected conventional modes of response and drew upon common intellectual resources to interpret their experiences. The social context remained important. As time passed, and as local communities assimilated the new religious culture, the exercises tended to become more ritualized, better learned, more habitual, and less intense. This development allowed the later naming, or taxonomy, of Stone and others. But at Cane Ridge, as in the early North Carolina revivals, the affected people had no clear habits to fall back on, no ritualized response. The descriptions therefore reveal enormous variety. Only one clear innovation seemed to mark Cane Ridge—what Stone would later describe as holy laughter or singing, coming from deep within the body. This exercise, noted by a few of the eyewitnesses at Cane Ridge, was suggestive of glossolalia and continued to be part of religious services at Cane Ridge and Concord for at least a decade.[28]

The reported excesses of the great revival splintered the Presbyterian clergy in Kentucky and Tennessee. The issues were very subtle. No one could blame people for involuntaty exercises, even when they were disruptive of religious services. And no one could ask ministers to desert people during such afflictions. All the ministers accepted pastoral responsibility toward their people, even when they had no personal taste for their wild behavior. At times the exercises skirted the bounds of Presbyterian propriety—women fell in unladylike positions, legs and breasts might be scandalously exposed, people in comas might become incontinent, men and women occasionally fell off horses, a few who fell in the dust or mud sustained minor cuts and bruises. At least at a distance some of the more frenzied dances bore an uncommon similarity to those in taverns; some bodily convulsions hinted at sexual congress. But it was clearly unfair to blame people for such appearances, as unfair as to indict these huge religious gatherings for the often scandalous behavior of spectators (largely involving drinking or coupling).

The issue that divided ministers was one of attitude and

28. Charles C. Ware, *Barton Warren Stone: Pathfinder of Christian Union* (St. Louis: Bethany, 1932), 187.

role. Most Methodists, and a growing number of Presbyterian ministers, not only accommodated the exercises but condoned them. Some used various techniques to stimulate them, believing they were an efficient means of converting sinners. The exercises were new means used by the Spirit in a glorious time of harvest. Always, or almost always, at the other end of the excruciating pain and remorse was unparalleled joy and happiness. It was all wonderful, almost miraculous, and they rejoiced in what was happening. They began to turn the adventitious into the expected. A special new revival culture was developing.

When Presbyterian ministers intentionally contrived such disorderly assemblies as that at Cane Ridge, their more cautious and skeptical brethren condemned them. In a sense they even drove them from the Presbyterian church. They did this because the new revival style so often subverted other Presbyterian norms—the balance of intellect and feeling in the individual's response to God, the proper combination of learning and experiential piety in the ministry, and, most determinate in the long run, the priority given to divine election (to God's will and choice) in conversion. Sooner or later, matters of religious style correlated with problems of correct doctrine. Together, these differences almost shattered the Presbyterian church in the West, leading to two major schismatic groups and eventually to two new American denominations. This is another complicated story, one that involves not only the events at Cane Ridge but their implications as played out in the revival's immediate aftermath.

CHAPTER THREE

Aftershocks

It is impossible to assess the significance of Cane Ridge apart from the whole series of great communion services in Kentucky in 1801. Because it was at least slightly larger than any of a dozen other very similar sacraments, because more people were affected with physical exercises than possibly at any other religious gathering in American history, and because of the extensive national reporting of events at Cane Ridge, it came to symbolize the great revival or even something as amorphous as a Second Great Awakening in America.

No doubt, Cane Ridge was a climactic event in one of the great religious revivals in all Christian history. In a six-month period in the central counties of Kentucky, the five to seven-day communions, with a growing number of families camping on the grounds, attracted a cumulative attendance of over 100,000 people, even by conservative estimates. Of course, numerous families attended five or six such communions, meaning that the number of people who came to at least one such sacrament may have been lower. But these figures exclude many people who attended Methodist quarterly conferences or protracted meetings in Baptist churches, where the crowds were smaller, the physical exercises more tame, and the publicity slight.

By the fall of 1801 evangelical visitors to the central counties of Kentucky marveled at a near utopia. The Spirit of God had burned and cleansed the whole area. Practically everyone had been somehow affected by the revival. George Baxter, when he arrived from the Shenandoah Valley, thought he breathed a special, cleansed air in Kentucky. He found "the most moral place I had ever been in," for he heard no profane expressions, everyone was amiable and benevolent, no private quarrels remained, and "a religious awe seemed to pervade the country. . . ."[1]

Despite the intensity of the Kentucky revival, it was still a local phenomenon. More difficult to assess was its national influence. The images of revivals as waves or flames spreading from some point of origin may mislead. Among Presbyterians, the revival began in the Carolinas in the summer of 1801, with the precipitating spark seeming to come from Logan County. Thus, if one seeks the point of origin, one has to turn to the work of James McGready. But of course to a large extent he only recapitulated the revivals of 1787–90, and one can keep going back to 1740 and then to Scotland and Ulster. In the Carolinas and in Georgia the great communions rivaled in size and intensity those in central Kentucky by the summer of 1802. None quite matched Cane Ridge, at least in the extent of physical exercises. But these communions to the east quickly became more ecumenical, with greater participation by other denominations, and because of the level of black participation much more interracial. Presbyterians often lost their dominating role, and by 1803 in some large union meetings in South Carolina they were outnumbered by Methodists and Baptists.[2]

Other strong centers of Presbyterianism—east Tennessee, central Virginia, the Shenandoah Valley of Virginia, and western Pennsylvania and adjoining areas of Ohio and what is now

1. Baxter to Archibald Alexander, January 1, 1802, in *Increase of Piety, or the Revival of Religion in the United States of America, et cetera*. (Newburyport, Conn.: Angier March, 1802), 63–64.
2. The most detailed account of the spreading revival, particularly in the South, is John Boles, *The Great Revival, 1787–1805* (Lexington: University Press of Kentucky, 1972).

West Virginia—shared in the revival. In east Tennessee the revivals began at least as early as 1801, often inspired by the same messengers who carried the news from Logan County back to the Piedmont of Carolina. In the western Pennsylvania area (the Redstone Presbytery) the first revival stirring came by 1799, but only after Cane Ridge did any communions rival those in Kentucky. One of the most effective ministers there, James Hughes, had success in 1799 and 1800, but then heard about the great revival in Kentucky from James Patterson. Hughes, like George Baxter, had come in the fall of 1801 to observe and to participate in three communions. Back home in Ohio County, Virginia (in the Wheeling area, just west of Pittsburgh), he was able to report comparable meetings as early as October, with up to 10,000 people, 750 communicants, and both camping on the grounds and plenty of swooning, just like in Kentucky.[3] In central Virginia the revival was not widespread until 1803, and seemed never as intense and affecting as in other areas.

Although New England evangelical journals avidly sought, and gladly published, every available bit of intelligence about the Kentucky revivals, it is not likely that they had much influence on the series of revivals that erupted in many areas of New England, New York, and New Jersey in 1800 and 1801. More of these were in Congregational than in Presbyterian churches, and the most lively in Baptist churches or in a rather thin scattering of Methodist circuits. And however extensive these eastern revivals were, they never rivaled those in Kentucky in physical exercises. Yet the affinities were significant, and by the 1820s Charles Finney led revivals (but not sacramental meetings) in upstate New York that rivaled in fervor those in Kentucky, including the number of people who swooned.

The intensity of 1801 could not last. Even in 1802 most Ken-

3. Letter from a person in Statesville, North Carolina, to David Jackson, 1802, in *Increase of Piety*, 107–108; letters from James Hughes, November 9, 1801–November 23, 1802, *Connecticut Evangelical Magazine* 2 (April 1802): 393–94; 3 (February 1803): 315–17.

tucky communions were less explosive than they had been a
year earlier. By 1805 Presbyterian ministers were once again
bemoaning the low state of religion in Kentucky. But their
perspective by then too easily betrayed the low fortunes of
Presbyterians in the midst of two developing schisms. Few of
the normally lasting benefits of a great revival accrued to the
Presbyterians. For the next twenty years, Presbyterianism in
Kentucky was moribund, barely growing at all, lagging behind both the growth in population, which more than doubled between 1800 and 1820, and even more the high growth
rates of the Methodist and Baptist churches. Whereas in 1800
the Presbyterians had approximately 30 ministers and around
2,000 members, in 1820 they claimed only about 40 ministers
and 2,700 members. The Methodists, with less than 2,000
members in 1800, claimed almost 21,000 in 1820. By then the
Baptists reported just over 21,000 members. And for both
these denominations, the great surge of growth came in the
revivals of 1801–1805, with the Baptists possibly doubling
their membership in 1801 alone.[4]

In the new century, evangelical Christianity clearly grew
more rapidly than the overall population in Kentucky. Even
the most bitter Presbyterian ministers confessed that, however much confusion and heresy reigned, the number of
avowed rationalists, deists, and skeptics shrunk toward zero.
The revivals also raised, at least briefly, the social conscience
of Christians. Antislavery sentiment became almost synonymous with revival, with the Cane Ridge congregation in
1801 filing one of the strongest antislavery petitions ever to
come before a Kentucky presbytery. The most fervent evangelicals also fought earliest and hardest for temperance reform, and struggled with eventual success to gain strong
Sabbatarian legislation.

In the view of many participants, the revival never ended.
Some Methodists and Cumberland Presbyterians talked of an

4. Robert H. Bishop, ed., *An Outline of the History of the Church in the State of Kentucky During a Period of Forty Years,* (Lexington, Ky.: Skillman, 1824), 253–58.

ongoing revival, one that might suffer temporary setbacks but whose overall direction was clear. Of course they used the term to denote not cycles of fervor or of successful proselytizing but an evangelical style. Those who were friends of the "revival" were those who worked, year in and year out, to increase the harvest. And from 1800 on the grain was always ripe somewhere. In any given year, certain camp meetings (now the main means of harvest) came close to the level of excitement of those hallowed ones of 1801. Itinerants and missionaries tried to extend the revival into new geographic areas, and the statistics on new congregations and new members each year testified to the continuing success of the revival. Its cumulative results were measured by the number of evangelical Christians in America, even though each person and each congregation had to suffer periods of deadness. The valleys were inescapable; the mountaintop experience was both rare and more treasured by that very fact.

The revivals divided Presbyterians but not Methodists and Baptists, who quarreled about several other issues. Baptists generally restricted their revivals to their churches or association meetings and continued to conjoin conversion, baptism, and membership in their congregations. They retained what they gained. Methodists tried to support a warm spirituality at all times. Their class meetings and love feasts, testimonials, hymn singing, and lay evangelism had many of the qualities of the Presbyterian communion. Since a revival style was normal, Methodists could join in the Presbyterian communions with alacrity, yet maintain greater order in their own, usually smaller conferences. In other words, both Baptists and Methodists easily adapted to the new revival style and made it an integral part of their religion. Methodists cried and shouted with joy in services throughout the year. This was normal. They rather easily accommodated more extreme swooning and jerking in such excited periods as 1801, but without making much of an issue of it. After all, John Wesley had preached so as to stimulate both the swooning and convulsions that always marked the greatest periods of revival among Methodists.

Presbyterians in Kentucky were less prepared to cope with explosive revivals. The church had long struggled to maintain a precarious middle way in doctrine, polity, and worship. It professed a Calvinism without the fatalism that some Regular Baptists (and most later Primitive Baptists) read into the doctrine of predestination. It stressed republican order as against episcopacy on the one hand, democracy or congregationalism on the other. It emphasized both reason and experience, the Word and the Spirit, in conversion. It carefully catechized its youth, yet expected them to suffer through the intense crisis of rebirth. Its ministers conducted ordered if plain worship services, keyed to a carefully argued and scriptural sermon, but often followed these services with warm and moving exhortations. As in any middle way, the pressure could come from both sides, from the ones who liked it hot to those who leaned toward formalism or calm reason.

In Kentucky, Presbyterian ministers were already divided by 1800 in temperament, in style, and in the understanding of such critical doctrines as divine election. In the dead years before 1800 they had suppressed differences as all prayerfully awaited a revival of religion. Even their salaries were at stake, for a majority of congregations defaulted on the promised subscriptions that allowed presbyteries to assign them a minister. The revivals forced all the old divisive issues into the open and added new heresies to perplex those who wanted to maintain orthodoxy, if anyone could determine exactly what that required. In the crisis the ministry lacked the political skills needed to navigate the shoals. As a result, two new denominations were born out of the revivals, both largely at the expense of the existing Presbyterian church.

Even in 1801 intimations of subsequent divisions gave a bittersweet flavor to Presbyterian rejoicing over the long-awaited revival. The great communions of 1801 continued almost weekly until the last scheduled one in November. With the last sacrament, the religious ferment all but ended for the winter of 1801–1802, revealing how fully religious excitement and conversions were now restricted to the communion seasons. Only a few "hot" ministers, such as Richard McNemar, managed to continue the revival, and report conversions, in the off-season, with winter activity centered in society meetings.

The diarist John Lyle tried to record the extraordinary works and to describe what he observed on the grounds. A young minister from Ulster roots who had been reared and educated in the Shenandoah Valley and who was partially deaf, he had only recently moved to a church near Paris, Kentucky, where he also became master of a female academy. During the winter of 1801–1802 he gathered his strength for another frantic communion season, which began with the first sacrament in April and did not end until the last one in early December. In 1802 most of these communions were smaller than in 1801, perhaps by design, since no one planned and organized any meeting on the scale of Cane Ridge. The number of cooperating congregations and ministers averaged only five or six, and the largest attended by Lyle featured just eight ministers. Only token Methodists and Baptists gave scheduled sermons (one or two at each communion), while Presbyterian preachers, when they had the time, gave sermons at Baptist associations and Methodist conferences. These smaller communions meant that home hospitality usually sufficed, with little camping. Unlike in the Cumberland area, Presbyterians in central Kentucky never adopted the camp meeting, in part because of the excesses of their New Light foes. But smaller meetings did not mean any abatement of the excitement or of the exercises, or preclude services that continued all night or at least into the early morning hours. People continued to fall, and conversions kept adding new members to the churches. The same pattern continued in the summer of 1803. Unperceptive lay people noted no change. But by then deep fissures in style and in doctrine had so divided the clergy as to spoil all the earlier fun. The exciting story of 1801 gave way to sadness and disillusionment among the Presbyterian clergy.[5]

Lyle suffered all the strains, and he alone left a record of his emotional highs and lows. He was capable of intense religious experience and at times knew something close to ecstasy, particularly during the communion. Possibly for the first time in his career he preached on occasion "with great liberty," departing from any text and following where the "Spirit led," often with a powerful effect on his audiences. He worked himself to the point of breakdown each summer, traveling to a joint communion at least every other week, there to preach and exhort and counsel for five almost sleepless days. Never had ministers in Kentucky faced as many demands on their time or as many erosive challenges to their egos. Even in ordinary times, the Scottish communion forced ministers to work in close concert, to follow each other in the pulpit, in effect displaying their skills before each other and before critical, demanding lay audiences. Such occasions undoubtedly stimulated careful preparation and as impressive performances as ability or inspiration allowed. But it was difficult to be up for each scheduled performance, particularly when services followed each other day after day. Comparison with more successful colleagues was sure to provoke self-doubt or even paranoia.

The revival atmosphere after 1801 increased the pressures on the professional clergy. The exercises quickly became the whole focus of attention. They became the evidence of an authentic revival, the mark of ministerial success. In the context, no preacher could fully resist the new standards, even when he viewed them intellectually as unfair or unscriptural. Lyle revealed his own deep ambivalence in his diary. As actor or performer, he could not resist a bit of self-congratulation when his sermons stimulated audience excitement, seizures, or—the supreme test—swooning. Yet he could not suppress his bitter-

5. Diary of Rev. John Lyle, 35–43, 57–58, 70–77, 98, 113–15, n.d., Manuscripts Division, Kentucky Historical Society, Frankfort.

ness, resentment, and anger when colleagues did not follow the rules, when they resorted to artificial means—shouting or crying in the pulpit, for example—to get the expected effects. He came to detest McNemar, who played on the emotions of his audience, even stomping his way among listeners when it seemed necessary to set them off. He also became disillusioned with lay people, whose poor judgment allowed them to fall for tricks or who at times seemed to make the exercises the end of religion. A subculture surfaced, one made up of people who wanted their religion hot, who seemed to come forward only at times of revival, and who accused Lyle of being against the revival whenever he talked about proper order or challenged the religious significance of exercises, which he did often by 1803.[6]

Lyle was not the first to urge caution and order. In September 1801, at the Walnut Hill communion, one of the largest after Cane Ridge, the venerable Rice preached against excesses, against too much noise and false exercises. To the gathered ministers he proposed a plan for regulating crowd behavior. Conventional in all ways, Rice urged elders to sleep between men and women whenever they gathered, in the early morning hours, in the meetinghouses. He also tried to organize elders to monitor the grounds at night, to prevent sexual liaisons or too much drinking (hopeful distillers had already begun a routine of hauling loads of whiskey to such mass meetings). Even such mild precautions offended a few of the emerging New Lights.

By 1803 deep enmities had developed among Presbyterian ministers. Sermons were worded so as to agitate doctrinal or stylistic differences, and veiled attacks on colleagues, or the fortifying of factional positions, seemed the point of all too many sermons. Certain ministers barely spoke to each other. The first open break came in 1803, but the issues dated back to the magical summer of 1801.[7]

6. Lyle diary, 35, 40–41, 45–55, 113.
7. Lyle diary, 44–46, 54, 113, 127.

The seeds of controversy first sprouted in the booming congregation of Cabin Creek (near Maysville, on the Ohio River), the site of one of the first great communions of 1801. Three elders of this congregation charged their minister, Richard McNemar, with heresy and tried to argue him back to Calvinist orthodoxy in Session meetings. When this failed, they petitioned the Washington Presbytery for relief. This presbytery, with only seven or eight ministers, included both northern Kentucky and new settlements across the river in what would become the new state of Ohio in 1803. Although neighboring ministers helped arbitrate the congregational dispute, it was clear that McNemar held firm to Arminian or free-will views even as he sanctioned the wildest exercises. More than any other minister, he precipitated what would soon be called the New Light or Christian movement. But no one was more fervent, more hopeful, than McNemar, and no one preached more stirring and affecting sermons. In fact, he almost lost his senses in the next three years, so intoxicated was he with the revival (echoes of James Davenport in the New England revivals of 1740).[8]

McNemar, who was of Ulster heritage, had grown up in a Presbyterian community in western Pennsylvania, accompanied Robert Finley to Kentucky, and settled with him in the Cane Ridge community. He gained his classical education in Finley's nearby academy. He early became an elder in the Cane Ridge congregation, and was one of those who accused Finley of drunkenness. Licensed to preach at Cane Ridge in 1797, he was subsequently ordained at Cabin Creek. After the first heresy charge there in 1802, he moved across the Ohio to the new congregation of Turtle Creek, near Lebanon. In this newly settled area, he and his much more subdued brother-in-law, John Dunlavy (also from Cane Ridge), became leaders of the most evangelical faction in a growing Presbyterian enclave. Since John Thompson, another young minister who had grown up

8. Barton W. Stone and Robert Marshall, "An Abstract of an Apology," in *The Cane Ridge Reader,* ed. Hoke S. Dickinson (N.p.: N.p., 1972), 151–53.

in the Cane Ridge area and studied under Finley, became minister of a growing church just outside Cincinnati, this area of southwestern Ohio became, in a sense, a colony of Cane Ridge, an outpost of the distinctive religious culture that had developed in that congregation.

McNemar's troubles followed him across the Ohio. Once again an alert elder detected his Arminianism and challenged him in the Session. Another fragile reconciliation in the congregation did not prevent McNemar's heretical views from becoming notorious among those who disapproved of his revival tactics. Matters of style as much as doctrine soon split the ministers in the presbytery. The presbytery met in Cincinnati in 1802, with McNemar's opponents in the majority. A lay delegate challenged McNemar's orthodoxy from the floor, leading to a presbyterial examination of McNemar. On his refusal to subscribe other than to the Bible, the presbytery found that he was indeed an Arminian and issued a letter warning the individual churches against his views. Nonetheless, the divided presbytery did not dare suspend him and even approved his half-time appointment at Turtle Creek, by then the largest Presbyterian congregation in Ohio. The next year, in a presbytery at John Thompson's Springfield church, the revival faction had a majority. This presbytery received a petition from eighty scattered church members accusing not only McNemar but also Thompson of unsound doctrine. It chose to ignore the petition and, to rub salt in the wounds of the protesting minority, approved McNemar as a full-time minister at Turtle Creek.[9]

McNemar's opponents had no alternative but to appeal to the new Kentucky Synod in its second meeting at Lexington in September 1803. By then it was clear that more was involved in the charges against McNemar than doctrinal issues.

9. Ibid., 154–61; Richard M'Nemar, *The Kentucky Revival or a Short History of the Late Outpouring of the Spirit of God* (Lexington, 1808; rpt. Joplin, Mo.: College Press, n.d.), 2; Barton W. Stone, "History of the Christian Church," *The Christian Messenger*, February 24, 1827, 78.

He was a spokesman for the extreme revival party in the church, and in his own congregations had moved far toward what his opponents saw as complete anarchy. Under the guidance of a few sympathetic Presbyterian ministers, the heady excitement and the bodily exercises of the summer of 1801 had not abated but expanded. As his enemies claimed, McNemar was not only an Arminian in doctrine but an antinomian or enthusiast in practice. It was as if all the heresies that had beset Reformed Christianity had invaded Kentucky and Ohio by 1803. These heresies would shortly include Arianism or unitarianism.

The synod had few alternatives. It had to censor the Washington Presbytery for finding McNemar guilty of Arminianism in one year and then approving his call to a church the next, and for not launching a full inquiry into the charges brought against him and Thompson in 1803. It also accepted the petitions against McNemar and Thompson and, instead of remanding them back to presbytery for trial (which was the normal procedure), moved to examine the two ministers on their doctrines. At this point McNemar and Thompson, joined by three sympathetic colleagues and friends, Barton Stone, Robert Marshall (one of the ablest ministers in the synod and pastor of a church just south of Lexington), and John Dunlavy, met, prayed, and then drafted a paper in which they protested the procedures of the synod and withdrew from its jurisdiction. In justification, they alleged that the charges against NeNemar were distorted and false. They claimed the privilege of interpreting scripture for themselves and placed it above all human-composed confessions. They thus endorsed McNemar's subscription to the Confession only insofar as it agreed with scripture. Furthermore, they alleged that some language in the Confession, that on election, strengthened sinners in unbelief and subjected the pious to a spirit of bondage. Since they could not hold these reservations without being viewed as disturbers of the peace and being called to account, and since they saw no future chance of relief from the synod, they withdrew from it but not from continued communion with the church.[10]

The synod attempted reconciliation at the same session. When this failed, it voted to suspend the five as ministers and declared their congregations vacant. It appointed a committee, chaired by John Lyle, to draft a circular letter explaining its action. The rebelling five considered themselves a separate presbytery, which they named Springfield (after Thompson's church). By this move they tried to maintain continuity with the action of the more friendly presbytery at Springfield a few months earlier.[11]

The five dissenters soon published an extended apology to explain their reasons for withdrawing from synod. In it Marshall developed a range of purely legal arguments to prove the irregularity, and thus the illegality, of the synod's action, particularly its suspending without trial ministers who had voluntarily withdrawn. Stone elaborately criticized the Confession, and thus the central tenets of Calvinism, taking for the first time, at least publicly, a fully Arminian position, one which involved quite deviant views on the atonement.[12]

The Springfield Presbytery remained in existence for only nine months. During this period its ministers met twice, once in a planned camp meeting, and without ordination accepted into fellowship two young ministers, a disciple of McNemar, Malcolm Worley, and a co-worker of Stone's, David Purviance. These actions only made more clear the almost complete dominance over the new movement of ministers with roots in the Cane Ridge congregation. In June 1804, at a final presbyterial meeting, six of the seven ministers (Purviance was present, not Worley) of the rump presbytery decided to dissolve, thereby eschewing all human titles and forms of

10. "Minutes of the Synod of Kentucky, 1802–1811," September 1803, in *The Presbyterians, 1783–1840*, vol. 2 of *Religion on the American Frontier*, ed. William Warren Sweet (New York: Harper and Brothers, 1936), 314–17.

11. Ibid., 314–19; Stone and Marshall, "Abstract of an Apology," 161–62.

12. Stone and Marshall, "Abstract of an Apology," 151–247.

church authority. Because this meeting took place at Cane Ridge, because five of the six ministers had ties to this congregation, and because the local congregation immediately joined Stone in declaring itself an independent Christian church, the Cane Ridge meetinghouse has ever since had a special status among the now-fragmented Restoration churches—Disciples, Christians, and Churches of Christ. The sturdy old building, stripped to its early log exterior and with the original gallery back in place, is now enclosed in a protective sanctuary and maintained as a historic shrine by the Disciples of Christ.

To their later embarrassment, the rebels justified their final break with ecclesiastical authority by a half-serious, half-whimsical "Last Will and Testament of the Springfield Presbytery" composed by McNemar. In it they proclaimed only one body of Christ and one church. They repudiated any central governing body for the church, made each congregation supreme in all matters of discipline and governance, dispensed with all creeds save the Bible, and expressed hope for a new era of redemption (a veiled reference to McNemar's millenarianism). At this point names became important. They adopted the simple titles of "Christian" at the suggestion of a visiting former Republican Methodist, Rice Haggard, who had helped form the first independent Christian churches in North Carolina in 1794, and who strongly advocated use of this name. The whimsy was reflected in a wry reference to those who had wanted to make the Springfield Presbytery their king, and in the expression of a hope that the Synod of Kentucky would examine all its members and suspend any who departed from the Confession, so that many could taste the sweets of gospel liberty.[13]

What followed this repudiation of all creeds and authority was a loose movement, at first centered on the Stone and Marshall congregations in the Lexington area, and on the

13. This Last Will has been published widely, but is in M'Nemar, *The Kentucky Revival*, 21–23.

This modern sanctuary now encloses and protects the Cane Ridge meetinghouse.

McNemar-Dunlavy-Worley-Thompson churches in Ohio. By 1805 the New Lights controlled about fifteen congregations. They also shared certain affinities with independent Christian congregations that preceded them in North Carolina and which were now organizing in New England. The New Lights effectively challenged Presbyterian orthodoxy in four areas. In fact, as the polarization proceeded, almost nothing remained in common to both groups save the most general Christian commitment.

The first challenge was to traditional, ordered forms of worship. All the early New Light congregations were faithful offspring of the 1801 revival. In fact, they carried it to its ultimate extreme. All the wildest excesses, plus open enthusiasm, blossomed in these congregations, making the label "New Light" a synonym of excess, something close to the unfair label of Holy Roller in the twentieth century. Stone, so reasonable in debate and so mild in manner, nonetheless presided over two of the wildest congregations in the greater

Lexington area. Visitors made clear that physical exercises, including frequent examples of swooning, became routine at Cane Ridge and Concord. A type of holy laughter suggestive of glossolalia survived there, perhaps alone, for a decade as a habitual even if involuntary part of worship. But the evidence suggests that Stone's congregations, and even more clearly those of Marshall, were mild compared to those of McNemar and Thompson.[14]

Worship in McNemar's congregations certainly had little resemblance to traditional Presbyterian order. The sermon seemed to shrink in importance or degenerate into pure exhortation. Church members stood and mingled in fellowship, with such violent hand-shaking as to vibrate the whole body. They engaged in mass confessions, prayer matches in which everyone prayed aloud at the same time, loud singing with hopping and skipping about, extemporaneous shouts or other voiced responses, and dancing. John Thompson, caught up in the frenzied hopes of the revival, made himself famous (or infamous) by dancing for over an hour around the tent at a great communion at Turtle Creek in 1804. McNemar loved all this, and wanted nothing to prevent the Spirit's moving at will among his congregation.

The ritualized and voluntary exercises diminished the need for but never replaced the involuntary ones. McNemar emphasized three of these, in addition to the falling. One was rolling, when people who swooned assumed a fetal position and rolled around like hoops. Another was the jerks, the most wild form of convulsions. Last was what he called barking. Under conviction, individuals seemed deliberately to debase themselves by assuming a doglike posture and growling and barking for hours. Several visitors observed numerous people acting like dogs. Even McNemar deplored this most degrading behavior, and attributed it to a reluctance to dance in worship. Beyond such exercises, McNemar embraced open en-

14. Joseph Thomas, *The Life of the Pilgrim* (Winchester, Va.: N.p., 1817), 154–57.

thusiasm—that is, he claimed for his flock several examples of direct spiritual inspiration. To him, the term New Light referred to the "inward light" that took precedence over scripture in the life of a Christian.

McNemar rejoiced in spiritual gifts, particularly prophecy (exhibited by the youthful exhorters in the revivals) and exorcism (the driving out of evil spirits from those lying on the ground), although he did not yet promote those of healing or tongues. He most valued the ecstatic visions that he claimed for many of his people when the soul left the body, often during a swoon, and they were caught up into the heavens. The sights glimpsed were holy, unspeakable. In their rapture, people communed with departed relatives, glimpsed the Holy City, and delighted in the smell of heavenly fragrances. For McNemar, such visions presaged the imminent return of Jesus to earth and the beginnings of some type of millennial kingdom. By 1805, as he reported it, the religious excitement, the sense of urgency and expectancy, had reached its limit. Something had to happen. Jesus had to come. Actually, three Shaker missionaries came from New York and very quickly persuaded McNemar to join them in a millenarian church.[15]

McNemar reflected an extreme position. Worley was no more circumspect. But Stone and Marshall never embraced visions and spiritual gifts, however many bodily exercises they condoned. When the Shakers came, and briefly impressed even Stone by their sincerity and simplicity, the New Lights were helpless. They had no confession, no denominational structure, no way of disciplining wayward brethren, no standards for determining what might be wayward. In retrospect, the early defection of the wildest brethren made possible the continued growth of the Christian movement. McNemar had led it toward a fanatical dead end. His excesses had embarrassed all the others, and the very label New Light became a burden.

15. These details come from M'Nemar, *The Kentucky Revival*.

The second challenge to orthodox Presbyterianism was much more difficult to counter. Here McNemar and Stone were in agreement, espousing a simple, egalitarian, and primitive form of Christianity like that practiced by the first New Testament churches. This position had a class bite to it. McNemar and Stone not only challenged any form of ecclesiastical authority but also most ministerial prerogatives. They stopped ordaining ministers, condemned the ministerial elite in existing churches, abolished subscriptions or other contractual forms of payment for ministers, and demanded that called ministers live simple lives, without finery or worldly distinctions. They drastically expanded the role of lay people in their congregations, and in many cases allowed new leadership roles for women, who made up a majority in their congregations. They did not advocate the sharing of goods, although McNemar later found in this Shaker practice one more tie to the first Christians. This primitivism had great appeal among lay people and continued as a central motif of the later Restoration churches. Otherwise, it is misleading to refer to these New Light churches as predecessors of the later Christian-Disciples movement, for in so many ways, beginning with the explosive conversions and the physical exercises and the spiritual gifts, the first New Light churches were closer to later Pentecostals than to contemporary Disciples or the Churches of Christ.

The last two challenges were doctrinal. In each case, the complexities do not allow any brief explication. The deeper but, as it turned out, more ephemeral challenge involved the most basic doctrines of Christianity—the ontological status of the Christ and the nature of atonement. Stone published his "heretical" letters on the atonement in 1805. In them he expressed doubt about the confused concept of three persons in a unitary god. He amplified these doubts in an address to the Christian churches in 1814 and then expanded on them in an almost scholarly debate with Presbyterian critics. His views would have enduring significance largely among those Christians who did not join Stone in the union with Alexander Campbell's Disciples of Christ in 1832.

Although frequently accused of being a unitarian, and at times even willing to use such a label for himself, Stone was in reality much closer to the ancient Arians. The orthodox Trinity formula makes the Christ one in substance with the Father, and thus in all respects a god. The Arians subordinated the Christ to the Father as a begotten son, but affirmed his pre-existence and special divinity. Stone found such a subordinationist position most reasonable and most consistent with scripture and thus adopted it. He believed that Jesus was the firstborn of God, created before time and any worlds, and that Jesus had all the fullness of the godhead in himself. Thus Jesus existed in spiritual form before his incarnation into a body prepared for him, a position made famous by the great hymn writer Isaac Watts. Stone argued that this position enhanced the divinity of Christ and avoided all the absurdities that accompanied the traditional but nonscriptural Trinity formula. Stone was not a unitarian, as most people used the label, for self-proclaimed unitarians almost always denied the divinity or previous existence of a fully human Jesus, however much they stressed the importance or divine inspiration of his mission. Stone's critics were often less given to precision than Stone, and liked to label him either a Socinian or unitarian. Presbyterians in Kentucky were almost paranoid on the subject since an English Unitarian, a follower of Joseph Priestley, had earlier come to Lexington to head Transylvania University, which Presbyterians had at first dominated.[16]

Stone also challenged orthodoxy by his views on why Jesus died on the cross. He could not accept the traditional Reformed understanding of the atonement, or the related concept of a God of justice and wrath as well as one of love and

16. Barton W. Stone, *Atonement: The Substance of Two Letters, Written to a Friend* (Lexington: Charles, 1805), 17–18; idem., *An Address to the Christian Churches in Kentucky, Tennessee, and Ohio*, 2nd ed. (Lexington, Ky.: N.p., 1821), 6–33; idem., *Letter to James Blythe, Designed as a Reply to the Argument of Thomas Cleland* (Lexington, Ky.: N.p., 1824), 6–47.

mercy. He also rejected the doctrine of complete human depravity. He particularly disliked the emphasis, in the Westminster Confession, on the legalistic appeasement of God's wrath, or the almost commercial idea that Jesus, by his death, assumed the debt of humans to God and "purchased" their salvation (substitutional atonement). Stone preferred a milder concept of God and a more loving atonement doctrine. Jesus, in his view, was the promised savior and mediator. He died in order to attest to the truth of God's promises and as the means of reconciling people to God, of making them at one with God (*atonement* meant "at-one-ment"). His death did not appease God's wrath but instead opened the way to salvation, and was a lesson in the type of obedience and holiness that is required for salvation. Thus, instead of the orthodox emphasis on the imputed righteousness of the Christ, which alone can reconcile people to God, Stone emphasized the real righteousness of Christians who follow the example of Jesus in suffering and sacrifice. Above all, Stone emphasized that Jesus' sacrifice was not just for the elect but for all humanity. He therefore embraced the central doctrine of Arminian or free-will Christianity—complete atonement.[17]

The fourth threat to Presbyterianism by the New Lights— their avowed free-will or Arminian position—was the most general and the most dangerous because it was the most popular. It is almost impossible to do full justice to the issues, even if one had unlimited space. The controversies were not new. They involved, at the surface, the issue of divine election and predestination, but more deeply the whole complex of Reformed doctrine. From their response to challenges posed in the early seventeenth century by the Dutch theologian Arminius, who believed humans could reject the grace of God, orthodox Calvinists had tried to make clear and to defend a conception of God and humanity, and thus of human destiny, that was as coherent as any vast doctrinal system could be, yet

17. Stone, *Atonement*, 3–35; idem., *Address to the Christian Churches*, 35–60.

so subtle, so precariously posed between the threatening abyss
of fatalism and the humanistic lures of free will as to confuse
even the orthodox. In time, it also involved a god and cosmology that were increasingly out of fashion and which seemed
unbelievably cruel to many honest people and incomprehensible to others. The Presbyterian church could not finesse these
issues. The strongest possible statement of these Calvinist doctrines was at the heart of their Confession. All converts, all
ministerial candidates, had to subscribe to this Confession
however well they understood the issues.

In the words of the Westminster Confession, God, who is
beyond all human comprehension, merits a long string of su-
perlatives. He is absolute, sovereign, self-sufficient, the foun-
tain of all being, infallible, and all-knowing. He is glorified in
all his creatures, needs none of them, does always as he wills,
and does all for his own glory. By his decrees, God willed that
some angels and people would inherit everlasting life, not because they deserved it (none do) but because he would work
salvation in them. The number to be saved is certain and defi-
nite, although known only by God. In the language of the
Confession, he chose these before the foundation of the
world, according to his eternal and immutable purpose, and at
his good pleasure. He did it freely, not because of foresight
about those who would render faith or good works or because
of any other purported merit in the creature. From the rest of
angels and humans, God withheld his mercy. According to
the unsearchable counsel of his will, and for his glory, as an
example of his glorious justice, he passed over these persons,
and made them objects of his wrath because of their sins. Since
God elected some to salvation, others to damnation, some
Presbyterians referred to this doctrine as double predestination, and it was clearly God's role in damning humans, not his
role in saving them, that created the greatest opposition to the
Confession.

The Confession clarified, and in a sense moderated, this
seemingly harsh position. It made clear that Jehovah ordains

all that happens, but usually according to secondary causes. His providence embraces even the fall of Adam (Adam acted consistent with divine providence). But Adam acted freely. That is, no natural necessity coerced his choice. People are free. They are also depraved. That is, their character, what they want, what they will, is ungodlike, and short of God's grace it remains such. Yet the Confession makes clear that God does not sin, is not the direct source of any evil (in their being, even humans are good, for only their will is depraved). Jehovah allows people to choose evil, allows even his elect to face temptation, but he does no evil. Finally, God works salvation indirectly, through various means. His Spirit works persuasively upon the will of depraved individuals, not by natural necessity. God gives people the ability to believe and trust. He makes it possible for them to respond to him in love. But since he works through their will and affections, the human response is voluntary, although such a response is impossible without illuminating grace and irresistible with it. To Presbyterians, these qualifications removed any hint of fatality in their Confession.

Their opponents did not agree. They also thought it inconsistent that these same Presbyterians, purportedly loyal to the Westminster Confession, could join so enthusiastically in efforts to win converts. Did they not always deny any human ability whatsoever to respond to God in full trust and love? Emphatically. But Presbyterians insisted that no one was damned because of any physical necessity. Literally, nothing stood in the way of anyone's salvation. But such were the sinful or rebellious affections of the human will that no unredeemed person could love God more than self. In this sense, everyone's character was corrupt or deformed, eternally separated from God unless God initiated the reconciliation. Salvation required a change of heart, a shift of basic preferences, a new character, a rebirth—all clearly beyond individual choice.

How does God bring his elect to salvation? Presbyterians insisted that he does not hit people over the head and drag them into the kingdom. Rather, he figuratively removes the scales from their eyes and enables them to see, really see, God and thus allows them appropriately, inrresistibly, to respond to him. How does he enable? By a linked, twofold means—by the invisible prompting of the Holy Spirit, and through a correct understanding of the Word of God as contained in scripture. Presbyterians saw great dangers in any severing of this linkage. Emphasize the inward illumination of the Holy Spirit, as did McNemar, and one flirted with enthusiasm or antinomianism, for in this case anyone could interpret the inward prompting however one pleased. Emphasize the Word, unillumined by the Spirit, and one moved toward an overly intellectualized and unmoving position which denied the necessary, immanent role of God and of his special grace (a position soon affirmed by Thomas Craighead in Nashville).

Because they assumed that people are free, Calvinists often lapsed into common language and spoke of human free will. But people are free only in the sense that they can choose what they like, not that they can choose their likes. Short of divine grace, what they like is always self-serving, God-denying, because that is how unsaved people always perceive their own best interest. Such a corrupt will, not itself an object of choice but the cause of choice, is in this sense never properly referred to as free. To so characterize it is to talk nonsense. In a moral rather than a physical sense, all human choices are thus determined. They are consistent with the will. In their natural, human condition, people simply do not have in their power any ability to choose God, or to choose with God, or to do what he wills. They have a contrary will of their own.

Then why preach at such people? Why plead with them to make choices that, in a moral sense, they are incapable of making? Why continually point out to them the horrible consequences of their godless choices? Such efforts seem to presume that people are able to make a personal decision to trust and obey God, when in fact morally they cannot do so. Until God transforms their will, they cannot choose other than they do.

But God has a plan of salvation. Through the Word and the Spirit God brings people to salvation, transforms their affections, gives them a new will. The transformed will is not thereby any more free than before; to suggest that it is is, again, to talk nonsense. But the will is no longer in bondage to self-love and pride. It is no longer sinful. Instead it is now tied to God's will, committed to his glory. And the choices one makes will reflect this new will—necessarily, but not from any physical necessity. The only reliable proof that a person has received such a new will is what the person chooses and does.

But one may still protest. The language of revivals was inconsistent with this understanding. For even Presbyterians urged apparently unsaved people to believe in God, to consent to God, to love him, and thus lovingly and willingly obey his commandments. To so urge is to suggest an element of choice, that sinners could respond to such a plea. Here there are indeed great subtleties, psychological as well as logical. What does it mean for a suitor to address a plea to his beloved—"Please, please love me?" She does not love him, else the plea is misplaced. And to love is clearly not a choice among options. Something ugly or repulsive is simply unlovable. But maybe, on occasion, the very confession of love, the voiced appeal to another, will so transform the perceptions of the beloved that she will, at that moment, see her suitor in a new way, find him lovable, and find in herself a reciprocating love. The heretofore unlovely suitor now appears beautiful. The very plea, absurd as it may be on its face, becomes a means of changing another person. It helps produce love, although this does not mean that love is a matter of choice. The same is true of endless sermons about God's love, and endless pleas for a reciprocating love toward him. Such sermons are God-ordained means to salvation. They make up the secondary causes that God uses to claim his elect. As they preached the Word—reiterated over and over again God's love as expressed through the Christ—Presbyterian ministers hoped their appeals and pleas, joined with the secret work of God's

Spirit, would produce a reciprocating love, that at some point the Word and the Spirit would enable the sinner to perceive God as he really was. This was the moment of grace. It invited thanksgiving, because those who perceived God would realize, as never before, and in a way never grasped by mere understanding, that they were in no wise deserving of such a reconciliation, and that no merit, no actions of their own, could in any way purchase such salvation.

Although love is not itself a choice, it produces choices. Thus, the new convert, although unable to choose love, does respond in love. The response, however one experiences it, is voluntary. One who loves does not remain passive or unmoved. Just the opposite. The evangelical appeal, for Calvinists, was not only a subtle appeal to love God, which only grace enables, but to do as love requires. Implied in the appeal was not only the immediate response but a lifetime of loving choices. Are such choices free? Again, the language borders on absurdity. The very meaning of choice is that people can do as they will, affirm their likes and dislikes. Choices are by definition free. But they remain within the context of will, of developed character, of likes and dislikes, and thus are tied to one's personal identity, not floating up in the air. The only meaningful sense of human freedom is not at all inconsistent with contextual or moral determinism, as the first great Calvinist philosophical theologian, Jonathan Edwards, so frequently argued, but are indeed inconsistent with mechanistic determinism. Also, for sinners or saints, human choice is in no wise inconsistent with an omnipotent God who wills all that happens in his universe, including all the choices that people make.

Given these often subtle distinctions, one can see why Presbyterian ministers preached revival sermons, and why Presbyterian sinners, to the extent they understood these doctrines, could appropriately respond to such sermons. But perhaps one can also understand why even Presbyterians might have difficulty with such subtle and precariously balanced doctrines. In fact, by the nineteenth century, it seems a majority of Presbyterians had problems with these very central and defining beliefs of their own tradition. Perhaps this is evidence that they had trouble living in a world so totally under the control of an all-powerful deity. Perhaps in a more humanistic age, in an America under a republican polity, such a God was no longer believable. As always, the theological workshops were turning out new gods, gods seemingly more benevolent, more obliging, and thus less awesome. In the religious competition, such new gods, like less demanding professors, almost always gained the highest enrollments.

Despite all the demurrals by Calvinists, Stone still found fatalism in the Confession. But what could he mean by fatalism? If he meant that God is in full charge of the whole show, and that all human choices are consistent with his will, then the Confession is clearly fatalistic. But if fatalism means that some physical necessity governs all choices, then it is not. Calvinists were clear on this. But they recognized the need to preach the doctrine of election with great care. If misunderstood, the unsaved could see in it a justification of their lack of faith, or believe that it presented an insuperable barrier to faith. But Presbyterians saw the election doctrine, however strongly worded, not as a stumbling block but as a consoling doctrine, for it placed one's salvation not on the precarious achievements of human beings but in the certitude of what God had decreed. Presbyterians also understood that election to salvation was only a necessary component of a complex of doctrines. For example, it is a necessary implication of divine sovereignty and human depravity, and makes clear that grace is irresistable, and that those elected to salvation, however many temptations they encounter along the way, or however low the level of their personal spirituality, are assured of their salvation.

These doctrines left an immense gulf between God and human beings. Salvation is never, in any possible sense, earned. This was a position that proved hard to swallow by many

Christians, particularly by the nineteenth century. Stone
could not accept it, for it meant that God, in a completely
arbitrary way, selects some undeserving persons for salvation,
but passes over other equally undeserving persons. Jesus'
death was efficacious for some, not for others. This seemed
horribly unfair. Even though, by the Calvinist system, God
was not the direct author of evil, he nonetheless ordained such
an arbitrary selection process and made the flawed vessels that
then became the object of his own wrath. Equally hard to accept was the fact that human beings were so helpless in the
whole scheme. Until the Spirit of God illumined their understanding, or removed the scales from their eyes, they could do
nothing to effect their own salvation. And when God took the
initiative, they could do nothing to resist.

Stone and his followers thus rejected the whole Calvinist
system. Like Methodists, they rejected each of the distinctive,
interrelated doctrines. In a sense, but in ways they would not
fully acknowledge, they changed their god. Stone could not
believe in a god of wrath and justice. He defined the essence of
his god as love. And he could not really accept complete human dependence. People retain a modicum of goodness and
have some initiating role in their own salvation. To make this
conception of god and humanity coherent, Stone would have
had to renounce divine omnipotence. He did not openly do
so. But consistent or not, his position was consoling to his
audience. His hearers welcomed a god of love who so desired
reconciliation with wayward but not completely depraved humans that he sacrificed his own son to demonstrate the depth
of his love. Such a god opened the path to salvation to all
humans who would accept it. He did not arbitrarily select
some. His grace was open to all, but it was not irresistible. It
was up to people to choose whether to believe in and trust God
or to resist him, and thus Stone, whatever the psychological
problems, made both belief and trust matters of choice. In the
same voluntaristic sense, Christians in Stone's mild form of
perfectionism could choose to obey God and remain faithful

to him, or else they lost the promise of salvation. Stone would still have insisted that human salvation is from God, a gift. No one can claim any credit for such a wonderful transformation, but all are responsible for how they respond to what God offers, and guilty when they reject such a wonderful gift. Thus, in a sense, salvation does have a moral quality about it, and God, in a governmental capacity, bestows salvation, not by arbitrary choice, but as a way of rewarding correct choices by his subjects.

Much could be said about the logical pitfalls, or the sentimentalism or incipient humanism, of such an Arminian position. To the limits of their ability, the Presbyterian clergy tried to use good logic to refute it. They enjoyed a rich heritage of anti-Arminian arguments, including the superb philosophical assaults of Jonathan Edwards. Two of the ablest ministers in the synod engaged Stone in extended debates after his letters of 1805. But from the first the Presbyterians were on the defensive. The New Lights always cast the controversy as one between the supporters of revival and those who opposed it. In vain Presbyterian ministers protested their zeal for a true revival. But as the controversies grew, they were placed in the awkward position of denouncing almost all the ongoing revivals, either because of disorderly exercises, purported dreams and visions, or heretical doctrines. Soon one of the ablest spokespersons for orthodoxy, John Lyle, became widely identified as an antirevivalist. In fact, only Thomas Craighead was by conviction and temperament clearly hostile to an evangelical form of Presbyterianism. Soon the synod, even as it tried to deal with the revivalists in the Cumberland schism, had to suspend Craighead from the ministry for his avowedly Arminian views. But Craighead came at it from the opposite side—a calmly reasonable, orderly, humanistic, mildly liturgical Presbyterianism, one shaped by eighteenth-century rationalism and close to the position of many contemporary Episcopalians. The New Lights were too hot, Craighead too cold. But how repudiate the extremes without seeming to be lukewarm?

Because of his age and his role in founding the Presbyterian church in Kentucky, David Rice became the most venerated spokesman for the synod. In a published sermon opening the annual synod in 1803, he tried to give a balanced evaluation of the recent revivals. Despite all that was happening, he was persuaded that Kentucky had enjoyed a great revival in 1801. Excesses were always part of such revivals and soon threatened their continuance. The enduring test of a revival was its moral fruits. All too quickly, Kentuckians fell into spiritual pride and began elevating other tests, such as joy and feeling and revelations from heaven. Thus, as he ruefully lamented over and over again, they had had a revival and then somehow mismanaged it. He itemized the failures—too great reliance on mere feeling, a partial emphasis on one ordinance over others (a dig at the Baptists), too little or too great church discipline, disputes between ministers and their flocks, an excess of physical exercises (no one could explain them, but they were at best incidental to the work of grace, at worst a delusion or diversion), a spectrum of new means and new doctrines, all manner of unfounded millenarian predictions, and many forms of disorder, beginning with immodest exhortations by women. In language reminiscent of Jonathan Edwards, he enumerated the evidence of a true revival—the prevalence of such ordinary means of grace as prayer, preaching, and singing; the humbled hearts of converts; the lively sense of God's presence; the concern for the salvation of others; and above all the reform of morals. He implied but did not emphasize a respect for established traditions and for the existing masculine authority system in the churches.[18]

In 1805, and again in 1808, Rice addressed epistles to the citizens of Kentucky, each a direct response to the New Light movement. In these epistles he defended key Calvinist doctrines, beginning with divine election, which when properly understood opposed fatalism and allowed free moral agency and various means of salvation. In a traditional Calvinist criti-

18. David Rice, *Sermon on the Present Revival of Religion* (Lexington, Ky.: Chapless, 1803), 2–27.

cism of Arminianism, he pointed out how the attempt to understand or make rational one mystery (how God chooses his elect) leads inevitably to a series of errors—complete atonement (more humane and reasonable), a benevolent and not wrathful god, a rejection of such mysteries as the Trinity and the atonement, a rejection of all miracles and mysteries, universal salvation (alone fair and loving), deism, and finally atheism. To his earlier itemized list of revival excesses he added the anarchy that comes from a rejection of all creeds and confessions. He tried to be fair. Even as he denounced, in 1808, the dangers of free-will perfectionism, he also indicted coldness and formalism and lifeless preaching.[19]

The New Light challenge faded a bit after 1805. No other Presbyterian ministers defected. The dissenters won most of their subsequent converts among Freewill Baptists. The movement first foundered when three Shaker missionaries converted the extremists—McNemar, Dunlavy, Worley, and a belated Presbyterian recruit to the new movement, Matthew Houston. The revival of 1801 was the basis of Shaker expansion to the West. At their home colony at New Lebanon, New York, the Shakers heard about the revivals in Kentucky, particularly the exercises and the ecstasy, and believed it would be fertile ground for their expanding movement. Three of their most persuasive missionaries, led by their ablest theologian, Benjamin Youngs, came to Kentucky and Ohio and addressed all the New Light congregations. Converted New Lights formed the foundation of the two earliest Shaker colonies in the West, Union Village in Ohio and Pleasant Hill in Kentucky.[20]

The United Society of Believers in Christ's Second Appearing, called Shakers because of their trembling in worship, had

19.   David Rice, "An Epistle to the Citizens of Kentucky, 1805"; idem., "A Second Epistle to the Citizens of Kentucy, 1808," in Bishop, ed., *An Outline of the History of the Church in the State of Kentucky*, 321–367.

'20.   Julia Neal, *The Kentucky Shakers* (Lexington: University Press of Kentucky, 1977), 1–7.

roots in both the early Quaker movement and in the charismatic French Prophets, who swooned in their mass meetings and then rose to prophesy about an impending millennium. The Shakers made up an avowedly enthusiastic sect, for its first great leader, Mother Ann Lee of Manchester, England, had claimed a direct inspiration from God, as had successive leaders of the movement. The formal doctrines of the group developed through time, with John Dunlavy later composing one of its major doctrinal statements. Mother Lee and eight disciples had fled from England to the American colonies in 1774. By 1780, following a fervent revival among New York and New England Baptists, she attracted a growing body of disciples, most of whom visited her at her home near Albany, New York. She died in 1784, leaving behind enough disciples to make up a large congregation. In 1788, a group of these Shaker families formed their first commune at New Lebanon.

As they developed their doctrines, the Shakers elevated Mother Lee from prophet to messiah. Her message of a new age, as understood by later Shakers, marked the beginnings of the millennium; it was only proper that the messiah this second time should take a feminine form in order to express the fullness of a mother-father god. The Shakers' antitrinitarian stance, their emphasis on a purely spiritual baptism, their advocacy of the gifts of healing, prophecy, and tongues, their loud and joyful singing, their visions, their contact with departed spirits, and their perfectionism all appealed to the most radical New Lights. As their order evolved the Shakers not only lived communally but, by mandate of Mother Lee, as celibates, since carnal procreation was inconsistent with the progressively developing millennial kingdom. They soon ritualized their spiritual gifts, notably in highly stylized and joyful dances that made up the most vital part of their worship. They were industrious, creative, simple, but never numerous, with a peak membership of 6,000 in a maximum of 19 colonies. Out of the western revivals came six of their colonies, four in Ohio and two in Kentucky. The New Lights converts,

McNemar, Dunlavy, Worley, and Houston, all became Shaker leaders, with McNemar the leading Shaker hymn writer and publisher.[21]

The Shaker defection, the lack of any order or discipline in the amorphous movement, and developing disagreements about baptism helped persuade Marshall and Thompson to return to the Presbyterian chuch in 1811. This left only Stone of the five original dissidents, and only him and Purviance of the first seven ministers. Stone only now assumed a primary leadership role in a very loose, very inclusive Christian movement, which soon informally bore his name (Stonites). He carried on an extensive correspondence and, in 1826, began editing the *Christian Messenger,* a semiofficial publication of the movement. Until after 1820 the small Christian movement grew slowly, with its greatest strength in Ohio and Kentucky, but with a scattering of small congregations in Tennessee and Indiana.

In time, Stone was able to bring some doctrinal unity to his movement. At first, only his atonement doctrine was distinct, but he never made its acceptance a requirement of fellowship. In fact, at first Stone welcomed diversity, and throughout his career yielded on almost every controverted issue in behalf of Christian unity. He early became a baptist (that is, one who endorsed the baptism of adult converts and, in the American context, by immersion) but would not make proper baptism a condition of membership. But by 1820 the movement was clearly baptist, and Stone was able to persuade several small Baptist associations to affiliate with Christians (no major doctrines, but only the issue of names, separated many Freewill Baptists from Stone). By 1820, as Stone indulged in more doctrinal controversies with Presbyterian critics, he elaborated a rather consistent free-will, or complete atonement,

21. [Benjamin Youngs], *Testimony of Christ's Second Appearing, Exemplified by the Principles and Practices of the True Church of Christ,* 4th ed. (Albany: United Society Called Shakers, 1856); John Dunlavy, *The Manifesto, or a Declaration of the Doctrine and Practice of the Church of Christ* (Pleasant Hill, Ky.: N.p., 1818); Neal, *The Kentucky Shakers,* 9.

profile of beliefs, with a unique conception of faith. He used the word *faith* for simple belief in the gospel message, one affirmed by reliable witnesses. Thus faith, in this defused form, came early in the drama of salvation. The Holy Spirit, in this scenario, was a gift to those with faith, not to those without. But the Spirit was a gift only to those who responded to the gospel, who obeyed its prescription of repentance, confession, and baptism.

By 1830 a related movement had spread from Western Virginia and Pennsylvania into Stonite country. This was a restoration movement first launched by a talented father and son, Thomas and Alexander Campbell. Thomas first immigrated from Ulster in 1807, while his son Alexander studied for a year at the University of Glasgow. Both were members of one of the Seceder sects of Ulster, and on arriving in America Thomas was briefly affiliated with a very small American branch of the Seceders, the Associate Synod. The old Seceders in America had all along vehemently opposed physical exercises and most emerging forms of revivalism. In background, style, and temperament, the Campbells were about as far as possible from McNemar and the New Lights.

In America, Thomas very shortly faced heresy charges before the Associate Synod and after complicated trials voluntarily withdrew from its jurisdiction. By his arrival in America in 1808, Alexander had also decided to leave such a strictly Calvinist church. The two joined in organizing an independent association, and soon an independent congregation, on Brush Run in extreme western Pennsylvania. Alexander lived on a farm just across the border at Bethany in the extreme northwest wedge of Virginia (now West Virginia). For almost two decades the Campbells joined their congregation to Baptist associations, first one centered in western Pennsylvania, then a more congenial association in the Western Reserve of Ohio. Joined by an able organizer and systematizer, Walter Scott, they gradually so reformed this association as to make it conform to what they believed to be the New Testament model.

In 1830, these Reforming Baptists decided to dissolve the association and to refer to themselves simply as Disciples of Christ (most outsiders called them Campbellites). Even before 1830, evangelists of the movement had successfully proselytized among Kentucky Baptists, thus often competing directly with Stone's Christians.

Alexander Campbell and Walter Scott matured the distinctve doctrines and practices of their restoration movement. Restoration is the proper word, for they professed no other purpose than the revival of the church of the New Testament, the one described in Acts and in Paul's epistles. The emphasis on a New Testament church meant, to Campbell, that Christians should follow in all details the new covenant and reject the old. None of the laws of the Old Testament applied to Christians, and any typologies or analogies from the Old Testament could not properly guide the church. Scott worked out an informed, reasonable, staged approach to salvation which bypassed the crisis conversions of evangelicals, and which by its very simplicity and lack of mystification proved a powerful proselytizing tool among confused people agonizing about their salvation. Campbell and Scott emphasized faith as no more than rational assent to the New Testament witness that Jesus was the promised Messiah, and stressed the remitting function of proper baptism (adult immersion). They were in the free-will tradition, affirmed complete atonement, and thus denied any curse based on original sin. But baptism formally remitted all penalties for actual, willful disobedience, and alone brought a person into the church. This "water salvation" became the favorite target of evangelical critics. Campbell's churches were also distinguished by weekly communion. Unlike Stone, Campbell argued that the Holy Spirit was a gift only to those who were baptized. Since the Spirit came after baptism, any reasonable person could believe and repent and thus come forward for baptism without any special divine initiative. His position was almost identical to the views of Thomas Craighead which had led to his expulsion from the

Presbyterian church. For the most part, Campbell did not share Stone's "heresies" on the Trinity, but by 1830 Stone was willing to deemphasize these divisive and, to him, nonessential speculations.

Representatives of the two movements, including Stone but not Campbell, negotiated an informal union in late December 1831 and formally ratified it at Lexington on January 1, 1832. In a sense, there was nothing to unite, because neither Stone's Christians nor Campbell's Disciples of Christ had any denominational organization. Tensions were inevitable, even over the proper name of the united movement. Many Stonites cherished their revivalist origins, continued to affirm Stone's Arianism, and resented Campbell's doctrinal rigidity and a few of his less than flattering remarks about Stone. In most regions the competing congregations eventually merged, but a remnant of Stonite congregations in the Midwest, joined by a small Christian movement in New England (an 1801 free-will splinter from the Separate Baptists), and independent Christian congregations in North Carolina and Virginia (survivors of the Republican Methodists) rejected union. More evangelical and often more "heretical" (many affirmed a unitarian position), most of these Christian Connection congregations merged in 1931 with the Congregationalists and are now part of the United Church of Christ.

After 1832, the Christian-Disciples movement grew rapidly. It soon became the major competitor with evangelicals in both Ohio and Kentucky (a few scattered Episcopal churches and a significant enclave of Roman Catholics in the Bardstown area offered little direct competition to evangelicals). The aging Stone had a declining role in the movement, even as his generosity had made possible a merger largely on Campbellite terms. Soon after the union he moved to Jacksonville, Illinois, and died in 1844 while on a preaching trip to Missouri. Although Stone sold his nearby farm and permanently moved away from Cane Ridge in 1812, preaching there only monthly from 1815 until 1822, he retained a special affection for his first congregation. On the second weekend of August 1843, the forty-second anniversary of the great communion of 1801, the venerable old man, at the end of his allotted three score and ten years, came back for a special meeting (communion was now served every Sunday), spoke briefly on Sunday, and then on Monday, the traditional thanksgiving day, preached his final, tearful farewell sermon. As he left the church grounds he paused, cane in hand, to point out the site of the preaching tent back in 1801. Stone requested burial at this beloved site. Three years after his death the Cane Ridge congregation disinterred his remains and moved them to the grounds of the meetinghouse.[22]

The New Light schism paralleled what turned out to be a much more damaging revolt within the Kentucky Synod involving the new Cumberland Presbytery. This revolt most directly involved the five ministers involved in the McGready revivals of 1797–1800. In this case, if the Kentucky Synod had not seriously erred in procedures and judgment, a denominational split might never have occurred. A majority of ministers in the synod, now deeply involved in the New Light controversy, mistakenly viewed the ministers in the more distant Cumberland Presbytery as concealed New Lights. In fact, none were as wild in style, as egalitarian in spirit, or as heretical in doctrine as McNemar and Stone.[23]

The McGready revivals created a temperamental split among the Presbyterian ministers in the Cumberland settlements. Caldwell's five boys, led by McGready, made up an evangelical party. They rejoiced in the revival harvest and worked to keep expanding it. Because of their very success,

22. Barton W. Stone, *The Biography of Elder Barton Warren Stone, Written by Himself, with Additions and Reflections*, ed. John Rogers (Cincinnati: James and James, 1847), 144; James R. Rogers, *The Cane Ridge Meeting House* (Cincinnati: Standard Publishing Company, 1910), 56.

23. The following account is drawn largely from two diametrically opposed narratives. The most detailed account and defense of the actions of the synod are in Robert Davidson, *History of the Presbyterian Church in the State of Kentucky* (New York: Carter, 1847), 223–56, while the most harsh condemnation of the synod and of Davidson's account is in Franceway R. Cossitt, *The Life and Times of Rev. Finis Ewing* (Louisville, Ky.: Woods, 1853), 325–478.

the synod separated the Cumberland district from the over-grown Translvania Presbytery in 1802. In the new presbytery, only Thomas Craighead of Nashville seemed a determined opponent of the revival faction, but after 1802 he and a few colleagues were consistently outvoted in presbytery. Even before separation, the Transylvania Presbytery, responding to desperate pleas from new congregations, had so relaxed normal Presbyterian rules as to license four young men without classical educations, including Finis Ewing and Samuel King, as exhorters or catechists. Whether they would have moved on to ordination is not clear.

In a series of presbyterial meetings in 1803 and 1804, the new Cumberland Presbytery proved willing to license, either as exhorters or preachers, every able young man who professed a calling, had experiential qualifications, and was willing to engage in an often very limited course of study and trial sermons. It soon had seventeen such candidates. Its presbyterial minutes often contained little else but the records of the new candidates. None of these candidates had a classical education, and those who so desired subscribed to the Confession with a reservation about predestination or with the qualification that they accepted the Confession only insofar as it agreed with scripture. The new presbytery also ordained three of the specially licensed young men, including the ablest and in time the most contested candidate, Finis Ewing, and in addition reaffirmed an earlier action of the parent presbytery and welcomed into ministerial fellowship the elderly Methodist missionary James Haw, who came from the by then defunct Republican Methodists. It seemed likely that, in due time, it would ordain all or most of the young candidates, a majority of whom had been converted or renewed in one of the great communions, which continued, with less excitement, in the years after 1801. Not only did the revival faction dominate the presbytery, but in a few years it might well have gained ascendancy in the whole synod.

The Kentucky Synod would later deem these young licentiates illiterate and incompetent. This judgment was unfair. By *illiterate,* representatives of the synod meant without training in the classical languages. The abilities of the young men varied. In native ability they probably matched, on average, that of the existing ministry, which overall was not especially talented. This circumstance may in part account for the emphasis so many of the older ministers placed on proper professional credentials. Some hints of class conflict surfaced in the controversy, but these young men were not at all rebels in the sense of a McNemar. In most respects they valued Presbyterian order and ministerial prerogatives. For many, ordination reflected a form of upward mobility.

Of all the "unqualified" ministers, Finis Ewing was most resented, particularly by Craighead. Ewing was probably the most talented of the group, and would take the lead in forming a separate denomination in 1810. A profile of Ewing easily dissipates the received image of the frontier enthusiast with none of the qualifications needed for the ministry. A large landholder and slave owner (he much later emancipated all his slaves as a religious duty) and a personal friend and later patronage appointee of Andrew Jackson, Ewing was the last child (thus his given name) of an influential Scotch-Irish family in Virginia. He married the daughter of the North Carolina revolutionary martyr, General William Davidson, and gained a thorough English education after moving to near Nashville. At first a member of a Craighead congregation in Davidson County, Tennessee (a county named for his father-in-law), he moved just before the new century to near McGready's Red River meetinghouse in Logan County, near present Adairville, Kentucky. In McGready's great communions, possibly the one at Red River in 1800, he experienced a spiritual renewal, became an elder in the Red River church (the Ewing family became the most prominent in the congregation), and soon presented himself as a ministerial candidate. By the time of his ordination he was arguably the most wealthy, socially the most prominent, and politically the most influential of all Presbyterian clergymen in the West.[24]

By 1804 the revival party so dominated the Cumberland Presbytery that a bitter Craighead and two other ministers petitioned the synod to correct several disorders. Most involved either the licensing of unqualified ministers or their assignment to preaching posts. The synod requested both sides to attend the next synod, and appointed an investigating committee that was much resented in the Cumberland area. It never did its work, leaving the issue for the synod meeting in Danville in 1805. Not a single suspected Cumberland minister attended. The synod thus had no means of acting, save in its normal committee review of presbyterial records. Such an examining committee, chaired by John Lyle, by now widely perceived as the most outspoken critic of revival excesses, found the minutes replete with examples of disorderly proceedings. Not only had the presbytery hastily licensed completely unqualified candidates, but it had licensed two from outside the bounds of the presbytery (the young men knew where to apply), had written letters requesting people to support illegally licensed exhorters, and, horror of horrors, had even in the minutes used the Methodist term *circuit* to refer to a group of churches served by Ewing. Confronted with the review committee report, the synod made a fatal error, one that jeopardized the future of the church not only in the Cumberland area but in the whole Southwest. Instead of instructing the presbytery to report on these charges, or to take specific actions to bring itself into conformity with the Discipline, the synod appointed a commission, vested with full synodical powers, to confer and adjudicate upon the errors found in the presbyterial minutes. The commission included ten ministers, all likely to be unfriendly to the majority faction in the presbytery, and six compliant elders. To rub salt into the wounds of the ministers

24. Cossitt, *Life and Times of Rev. Finis Ewing,* 22–64; Finis Ewing, *Lectures on Important Subjects in Divinity,* 3rd ed. (Louisville, Ky.: Morton and Griswold, 1854).

of the targeted presbytery, it was chaired by Lyle, who was in no position to be impartial.

John Lyle prepared himself well for the commission hearing. He spent the prior two months (October and November 1805) on a preaching mission to the Cumberland Presbytery. He preached in every major church in the Cumberland, officiated at communion services, took part in one camp meeting, and rode horseback for long hours to reach outlying churches, accompanied at times by McGready, Hodge, McGee, or Rankin. The collegiality was a bit strained as the serious, conscientious Lyle argued both doctrines and practices with his colleagues. He was not happy with much that he found in the Cumberland. Disorder seemed the norm—he met a Negro exhorter who danced wildly as he preached, heard one young licientiate urge a congregation to shout and jerk, found only McGready consistently orthodox in doctrine, and almost despaired when Craighead, the one advocate of order, proved a Pelagian in his beliefs. In one respect only he slightly moderated his animus against the young men. They were indeed illiterate, without classical knowledge. At least one did not seem to have even a good English education (his grammar was atrocious). But these earnest young men were not New Lights. Lyle heard many of them preach coherent sermons, ones well matched to their audiences. None were clearly enthusiasts (they did not rely on visions or any special inspiration directly from God) or antinomians (none claimed such sufficiency in grace as to ignore the proper means of salvation or conventional moral codes). But they were, to a man, Arminians and crypto-Methodists. As he moved to Gasper River for the opening of the commission on December 3, Lyle was clearly open to compromise on the educational deficiencies of the young men, but not on their flagrant free-will heresies. Had the young men been willing to subscribe the Confession and satisfactorily answer detailed questions about doctrine, the commission might well have accepted their licenses and even agreed to their eventual ordination.[25]

A quorum of the commission made it to John Rankin's Gasper River meetinghouse by December 3. The ministers of the Cumberland Presbytery were instructed to attend in order to ensure a "full, fair, and friendly investigation." Over half came, but the commission found itself in completely hostile territory. No one wanted to board the commission members, who had to suffer through each hearing day without food. Lyle did not help by preaching a three-hour opening sermon on the needed qualifications of ministers. The commission assumed the right of examining each of the young men, including the three ordained ministers, and asked that they all appear by name and submit to questions. After prayerful deliberations in the woods, none of the young men submitted, largely because of instructions from their venerable mentors, McGready, Hodge, McGee, Rankin, and McAdow, who argued the illegality of the proceeding, for only a presbytery had authority to pass on ministerial qualifications or to remove ministers on the basis of charges of heresy or misconduct. The Presbyterian General Assembly later agreed with this judgment.

The commission, which was much more concerned about Arminianism than a lack of Latin and Greek, rendered a harsh verdict. It suspended the ex-Methodist Haw from the ministry until he submitted to examination; suspended all twelve young men who publicly refused to submit to examination, including the already ordained Ewing and King; suspended twelve absent licentiates until they submitted for examination; and brought charges of contumacy or heresy against the five older ministers. Lay people in the Cumberland area saw the proceedings as an illegal inquisition, an attempt to take away their beloved ministers simply because they supported

25. "A Narrative of J. Lyle's Mission in the Bounds of Cumberland Presbytery," 5–28, 56, 57, n.d., Manuscripts Division, Kentucky Historical Society.

the revival, placed the Bible above creeds, and had had no opportunity to study Greek and Latin.

In a brewing rebellion, the commission's action was about as likely to produce reconciliation as the Intolerable Acts before the American Revolution. Since it acted for the synod, none of its decisions had to be approved at the next synod. But the synod had to take up the cases of the five ministers cited to appear (McGready and McAdow for resisting the commission; Hodge, McGee, and Rankin for holding false doctrines as well). Meanwhile, the ministers in the Cumberland Presbytery had carefully calculated their strategy. All the young men continued to preach, else over half the pulpits in the presbytery would have been vacant. Their suspension made them, if anything, more popular and more effective. The ministers and elders who normally met as a presbytery now met as a council. It assigned its technically unfrocked ministers and licentiates, but did not license or ordain new people. The five cited ministers did not accept the legality of the commission's charges and did not come to synod for trial. But the group sent Rankin and Hodge as spokesmen to the synod, with some hope of concessions and reconciliation.

The split was particularly distressing to McGready and Hodge. Now older men, fathers of the revival, mentors to half the young men threatened with loss of their careers, they remained loyal to their Presbyterian heritage and, at least in the case of McGready, fully orthodox in belief (McGready supported those who could not subscribe fully, and did not want to make this issue so important as to impede the revival). But McGready was in no position to mediate by 1805. He suffered a distressing dispute about land in Logan County, and two years later would accept a call to a congregation he had helped form back in 1800, in Henderson, Kentucky, on the Ohio. He subsequently explained his absence from the synod meeting of 1805 and was never challenged again for any of his actions. In Henderson he enjoyed a quiet and peaceful ministry until his death in 1817.

At synod, a special committee conferred at great length with Rankin and Hodge. The synod was stuck with the high-handed action of its commission and could do no other than uphold it. But it wanted reconciliation. Hodge and Rankin conceded on one issue—they would submit to examination on their doctrines. Hodge, at least, submitted in good faith, for in 1809, on the verge of final separation, he adhered to the traditional church, reluctantly deserting his Cumberland brethren. Rankin's concession is harder to explain, for he had seemingly held a more Arminian position. What Hodge and Rankin would not concede was the legality of the suspension ordered by the commission. They would not desert the young men back home. For their efforts at reconciliation, and because they were present, they suffered the consequences. The synod suspended them from the gospel ministry until they submitted to its authority. In addition, it abolished the Cumberland Presbytery, moving its few loyal ministers back to Transylvania. For Rankin, this suspension turned out to be the final blow. Already impressed by Shaker missionaries (who came to the commission meeting at Gasper River with a hope of exploiting the impending schism), he converted in 1807 and used his farm to begin a new Shaker colony, South Union, about a mile and a half south of his Gasper River church, which eventually would be enclosed by the 6,000 acres owned by the colony.

The failure of reconciliation efforts at synod left an impasse. The Cumberland Council appealed its case to the General Assembly in 1807 and in effect won on procedural grounds. The commission had erred in a dozen ways. In some cases its actions were simply uninformed—it indicted the Cumberland Presbytery for admitting Haw and licensing Ewing and King, all actions of the Transylvania Presbytery. But the crucial error was its assumption of illegal authority. A synod, or an agent of the synod, could not act against individuals except by appeal from a presbytery. It could not suspend licentiates or ministers except for cause, and even then not without charges in presbytery. The assembly requested the synod to review its questionable procedures in the suspensions and even urged it to take steps to restore the Cumberland Presbytery. At the same time, it wrote to McAdow its concerns over the relaxation of educational and doctrinal standards by the former presbytery.

By now reconciliation was impossible. The synod would not give an inch, even risking insubordination to the assembly. Instead of reviewing the work of the commission it wrote a lengthy defense of it, but by inadvertence failed to get the response to the General Assembly of 1808. This assembly, which had received another appeal from the council, seemed prepared to declare the whole commission contrary to the Discipline, and thus nullify its actions, but would not act in the absence of any report from the synod. In 1809 the synod sent not only its defense but also John Lyle to argue it before the assembly. Lyle made a passionate, even tearful plea for the upholding of order, and gained a unanimous vote to sustain the synod.[26]

This action ended almost all legal avenues open to the Cumberland Council. In 1809, in an informal offer to the synod, it accepted examination of the suspended ministers on doctrine, but only if they were restored to their former status as conferred by the Cumberland Presbytery. They were also willing, as a group, to adopt the Confession, with the only exception involving fatality. The synod rejected such collective restoration and at first considered a special committee to examine each individual, but then remanded the task to the Transylvania Presbytery, which convened a special meeting for the examination. William Hodge, Hodge's nephew, and one other young licentiate came and subscribed the Confession. Hodge was thus readmitted to the ministry. Since the two younger men had been "irregularly" licensed, they sub-

26. *Minutes of the General Assembly of the Presbyterian Church in the United States of America, 1789–1830* (Philadelphia: Presbyterian Board of Publication, 1847), 378, 383, 389–90, 392–93, 408–409, 416.

mitted to an examination and were admitted to candidacy, with no protest about their lack of a classical education (the younger Hodge was one of the least educated of the group).

By 1810 the small remnant of ordained ministers in the old Cumberland Presbytery faced some hard decisions. Most of the young men had never been ordained, and thus had no legal standing in any denomination. On principle, most of the young men would not yield to the synod, and on doctrinal grounds could not in good conscience give unqualified submission to the Confession. They were all part of the new revival culture, committed to an experiential religion, to fervent preaching, to the new camp meetings, into which they were blending the old Scottish communion. But they were not New Lights. As far as the record reveals, none either placed undue influence on physical exercises or in any way relied on visions or dreams. They remained orthodox on the doctrines of the Trinity and the atonement. They accepted Presbyterian order, as against Baptist congregationalism or Methodist episcopacy. On Calvinism, they were ambivalent but generally positive. They would have none of Stone and McNemar's wholesale repudiation. Perhaps William McGee best reflected their dilemma. McGee hoped to forge a position halfway between Calvinism and Arminianism—a heady task indeed, but one that must have appealed to most of the young men. As it turned out, they would continue to affirm the divine initiative in salvation, but make grace in some sense resistable. They believed in a conditional atonement, applicable only to those gifted with faith, but somehow believed it was available to all. They accepted autonomous choice in salvation, but held on to the consolation of perseverance ("once in grace, always in grace").

By 1810 the ordained ministers still in suspension, Ewing and King, had the support of only two of the older ministers, McGee and McAdow. But of these four, McGee was ambivalent, not yet willing to leave the church of his childhood to form a new denomination. And McAdow was over fifty, had long been infirm, and was officially retired because of ill health and a weak speaking voice. King was not particularly able. Thus, the leadership of the group devolved on the capable but by then completely rebellious Ewing. He was determined to separate completely, and later avowed he would have taken the step even if two other ministers had not joined him (in the Presbyterian system, it takes three ordained ministers to constitute a presbytery). By February 1810, Ewing had persuaded McAdow to join, and he and King met at McAdow's log house in Dickson County, Tennessee, to form an independent Cumberland Presbytery. For the Cumberland Presbyterians, this became a hallowed event, their declaration of independence. McGee soon joined the new presbytery, and he and McAdow drew the expected suspensions from the Kentucky Synod. The new presbytery was now free to license and ordain all the young men who had been in a state of ecclesiastical limbo since 1805. It long continued to ordain ministers with limited formal education, but in accordance with the covenant that the three founding ministers had written at McAdow's cabin, the new church encouraged prospective ministers to gain as much education as possible and listed requirements in all areas save the classical languages.

By 1813 the Cumberland Presbytery had over sixty congregations, most still in the Cumberland area. At the presbyterial meeting of that year, the assembled ministers formed a Cumberland Synod, divided its churches into three presbyteries, and appointed a committee to draft a confession. The new synod approved the confession in 1814. It was very much the hybrid that McGee had wanted, a blend of Calvinism and Arminianism. Except on the issues of election and reprobation, it followed the Westminster Confession. But in some treacherous logical hairsplitting it repudiated double predestination (God has not eternally decreed the damnation of anyone) and affirmed complete atonement (the Christ died for all people), which removed any blight of original sin from infants. Of the traditional five points of Calvinism, it kept only perseverance.[27]

After 1814, the new Cumberland church expanded rapidly (it formed a General Assembly in 1829) through most of the trans-Appalachian West, into the Midwest, and to California. In polity it remained presbyterial, in doctrine hybrid, in style as evangelical as Methodism. The Cumberland presbyteries utilized rural circuits much as Methodists did, formed camp meetings in new areas as proselytizing tools, and emphasized revival techniques. Even by 1820 the new denomination vastly outnumbered regular Presbyterians in the original Cumberland region, and had almost half as many members in Kentucky as the parent church. It expanded mostly by missionary efforts, not by absorbing older Presbyterian congregations. In the West it soon reflected the more evangelical version of Presbyterianism, and by the polarizing effects of the schism drove the older Presbyterians further away from new revival methods, thus helping ensure the virtual stagnation of the old synod. East of the Appalachians most evangelical Presbyterians remained in the old denomination, making up a distinct faction.

During the nineteenth century the issues that led to the Cumberland rebellion became less critical. After 1880 the Cumberland Presbyterians began merger discussions with the northern Presbyterian church. In preparation, the Presbyterian Church in the United States of America so modified its confession as to accommodate the Cumberlands; it virtually accepted complete atonement and affirmed the salvation of all infants. In 1906 both bodies voted to merge, which in most respects meant the absorption of the smaller, more southern Cumberland Presbyterians. For several reasons, approximately one-third of the Cumberland Presbyterians re-

27. *The Confession of Faith of the Cumberland Presbyterian Church in the United States of America* (Nashville: Cumberland Presbyterian Board of Publication, 1879).

jected merger and have continued as a small, still disproportionately rural, evangelical denomination largely in the
mid-South. In a sense, these surviving Cumberland Presbyterians represent the closest living link to the revivals that began with McGready in 1797.

Institutionally, any survivals of the great Scottish-type communions of 1801 are few or indirect. Among the more evangelical Presbyterians in the East, and above all among the
Cumberland Presbyterians, the extended communion gradually blended into the camp meeting. The most frequent pattern even of Methodist camps remained that of the old communion—from Friday to Monday or Tuesday. But the sacrament gradually lost its centrality, although any Cumberland
Presbyterian camp even by the mid-nineteenth century still
featured communion on Sundays (Methodist camps also had
communion services). But more traditional Presbyterians re-
sisted camps and tried for at least another generation to preserve the Scottish sacrament.

The first casualty of the new century seemed to be the tokens, which were less and less used after 1800. Presumably the
careful prescreening of members, the Protestant version of
confession, ended along with the use of tokens. But only
much local church history can trace such institutional
changes, changes that usually take place more slowly than one
might anticipate. As late as 1820 one can find plenty of references to weekend communion, apparently of the old Scottish
type, attended by several local ministers. These seem to have
shrunk to three-day or even two-day affairs. It was only one
more step to communion Sundays with only a few guests
from neighboring congregations. What is unclear is how soon
most Presbyterians gave up the seating at tables and began
passing the attenuated elements along the pews. Whatever the
process of change, by mid-century such older Presbyterian
ministers and scholars as William Foote and Robert Davidson
referred back to the old communions with nostalgia, and

tried, perhaps without success, to explain them to a new and uncomprehending generation. Maybe, somewhere in America, some rural congregation still celebrates the old communion, but, if so, such a sacrament has become a souvenir of a past age.

Some Conclusions

In the history of Christianity Cane Ridge remains a small but prominent landmark. In the history of Reformed Christianity in America it is much more than this, justifying several contemporary descriptions of it as the American Pentecost. In it one can glimpse some important continuities in the single most important confessional tradition in America—a tradition somewhat misleadingly called Calvinist. If anything, I have overemphasized traditions, some doctrinal, some institutional. More than any prior historian I have focused on the sacramental aspects of Cane Ridge, and thus the area of greatest continuity with the past, even as I found little reason to emphasize environmental influences, particularly that of the frontier. But in this microcosm of evangelical Christianity, I hope I have adequately stressed some new departures—the confusing erosion of basic Calvinist doctrines and the emergence of such new institutions as the camp meeting. By *evangelical,* I simply refer to those branches of Christianity that required, and made central, an arduous, crisis-like conversion, and that, subsequent to this climactic experience, emphasized a warm, spiritual, affectionate form of religion.

To structure some conclusions, I return to my opening taxonomy of religions. I here shift my focus, at least to some extent, from what I see as most central and distinctive in Christianity—a concern for correct belief and a desire for salvation—to three subordinate but still critical character-istics—rituals, moral demands, and ecstatic experience.

To a much greater extent than I imagined when I launched this study, Cane Ridge demonstrated the continued impor-tance, but also the increasing vulnerability, of the sacraments in Reformed Christianity. The two original sacraments of the church—baptism and a communal meal in memory of the Last Supper—not only continued to have an important place in Protestant worship, but for Scottish Presbyterians the com-munion meal also provided the main vehicle for renewal or revival. For both Baptists and Methodists the two sacraments were vital but varied somewhat in significance from one de-nomination to the other.

Because the baptism of infants remained normative for Methodists and Presbyterians, yet without any remitting function, the sacrament had no immediate tie to conversion or church membership. But it continued to be a crucial sacra-ment for parents, who believed that the congregational com-mitment made to infants as they became part of the conve-nanted community increased the likelihood of a later rebirth experience (by the effect of Christian nurture for Methodists; according to the likely design of God for Presbyterians, who saw baptism as a sign of the covenant of faith and a Christian substitute for circumcision). For almost all Baptists, whatever their doctrinal disagreements, the baptism of adult converts was so critical, both as a first act of obedience and as a symbol of the death of the old person, as to be logically, not causally, a part of what it meant to be converted. The later Christians-Disciples took this position all the way; by their emphasis on baptismal remission they fully reintegrated conversion, bap-tism, and church membership, even as it has always been inte-grated in the Roman Catholic Church. But because of that very reintegration, they deemphasized a crisis conversion and thus moved beyond the boundaries of evangelicalism, as I have defined that ambiguous term. For both Baptists and Dis-ciples, the mass baptism of converts along rivers and creeks became one of the most intense and fulfilling religious occasions in America, not only a time of rejoicing, of renewal and revival for Christians, but an especially convicting time for those outside the church.

The role of communion raises much more complicated problems. Until Cane Ridge, the great Scottish communions remained for Presbyterians not only the highlight of the church year but the main institutional vehicle for conviction and conversion. The sacramental season and revival were almost synonymous. Clearly, the communion service was not as central, and not so tied to conversion, among Methodists and Baptists, although their conferences and association meetings usually climaxed in a communion service. But it seems reasonably clear that, by the time of Cane Ridge, the sacrament was already losing significance for almost all evangelicals, and that new revival techniques, some already in evidence at Cane Ridge, hastened this erosion. That is why I said, at the beginning, that Cane Ridge was not only the greatest Scottish communion in America but in a symbolic sense also one of the last.

Long before Cane Ridge, the meaning of the communion service had already shifted among most Protestants from the understanding of the early reformers. Among Lutherans as well as in most Reformed confessions, the sacrament became primarily symbolic, a reminder of Jesus' passion, and because of scripture and tradition, the most important ritual or ordinance in the church, but not different in kind from other ordinances. For the reformers, the communion clearly stood alone, almost as much a miracle and a mystery as it had been for Roman Catholics, even though both Luther and Calvin tried to strip from it the magic and superstition they saw in the Catholic Mass. For Calvin, the doctrine of the real spiritual presence of the Christ in the supper, and the sense of a precious unity with the Christ, bodily as well as in sentiment, made the sacrament a uniquely powerful ritual, not a mere symbol or a sign of grace. Among both English Puritans and Scottish Presbyterians, this highly sacramental emphasis clearly declined by the eighteenth century. One way of stating this is that Reformed Christians had moved ever further away from the Church of Rome, or from a Christianity tied closely to church and sacraments.[1]

By Cane Ridge, new revival techniques were further eroding the centrality of the communion. They began to detach conversion from any necessary tie either to the communion table or to church membership. In the old Scottish church, the great communions meshed well with the ordinary rites of passage, the techniques used to train children and bring them to confirmation. After catechism came confirmation and first communion, or what became the climax of a process of conversion, one indeed attended with deep feeling but not necessarily with the devastating crisis that became normative in 1800 in the more evangelical churches. After confirmation, the communion came closest to recapitulating the intense feelings that were supposed to mark the rebirth experience.

For envangelicals, the peak religious experience of a lifetime—conversion—came only once. This created a dilemma. Early Methodists, as well as later holiness sects, added a second climax, tied to sanctification or the baptism of the Holy Spirit. But even this second peak left long years when it was difficult for Christians to retain, or regain, the intense experience of these climactic moments. Several rituals or ordinances helped—group prayer, tearful confessions, baptisms, vicarious participation in the conversion of others, all the way down to such particularizing ordinances as foot washing or love feasts. But at least for Presbyterians the traditional, highly

---

1. Few American evangelicals challenged the trend away from sacramentalism. The exceptions were two theologians at the first seminary of the German Reformed Church in America, Philip Schaff and John Nevin. The seminary eventually settled at Mercersburg, Pennsylvania, and lent its name to the theological outlook expressed by Schaff and Nevin. They wanted to reclaim for their church the strong sacramental emphasis of Calvin. In two polemical essays published as a book, *The Anxious Bench* and *The Mystical Presence* (Chambersburg, Md.: n.p., 1843), Nevin indicted the new revival methods and the demotion of the communion to a mere symbolic ordinance.

sanctioned, and most appropriate ritual of renewal remained the communion, which in its entirety, with all the preparations and follow-ups, reinforced communal unity and recapitulated not only the passion of the Christ but each person's own rebirth experience (self-examination and conviction, penance, and joyful release). It was also a powerful convicting ordinance for those outsiders who could only observe the sacrament from their pews.

The unanswerable question is whether the sacrament of communion still had this centrality, still had this meaning, for those who came to Cane Ridge. One can doubt it, except for a minority of older Scotch-Irish Presbyterians who continued to honor the old religion—a religion by then neglected by the uncomprehending multitudes. For most people on the grounds the deep sense of conviction, the agonizing struggle to "break through" to comfort, seemed scarcely related to the communion service. It was as if two parallel processes went along simultaneously—the communion for the traditionalists, new revival techniques for everyone else. These revival techniques involved new rituals—new hymns and new modes of singing them, lay exhortation and personal pleading with identified sinners, and special locations at the front of the church or before the tent where those under conviction came for special prayers and focused attention (these places were called mourner's benches in the Cumberland revivals, and later made famous as the "anxious bench" by Charles Finney). It is ironic that, much later, American evangelicals would identify these rituals as part of the "old-time religion" when in fact almost every technique involved innovations rooted neither in church tradition nor in scripture.

The innovations soon became valued rituals, repetitious and familiar. The gradual erosion of the traditional sacraments did not mean a diminished importance of rituals, just a shift in their form. Such shifts were not necessary to produce an evangelical version of Christianity. John Wesley demonstrated that a warm, spiritual religion is as possible in a high church, liturgical tradition as within the more plain and simple style of Puritans and Presbyterians. The formal aspects of worship do not correlate, in any one-to-one way, with the emotional tenor of church life. The most ecstatic or charismatic religion is consistent with a highly formal or ritualized setting, even as a cold and lifeless religion is consistent with a plain meetinghouse and worship services largely keyed to the sermon. It all depends on the meaning the forms have for participants.

Any style of worship is open to formal analysis. Any religion, if it endures through time, will develop rituals. The beloved hymns of early Methodism, tied to such innovations as confessionals and love feasts, all constituted new liturgies, as complex and soon as familiar and fulfilling as the rather formal and often ignored liturgy based on the *Book of Common Prayer* that John Wesley sent to America as a guide to Methodist worship. It is also conceivable that some of the new forms were as complex, as intensely involving, and as broadly responsive to a variety of human needs as the old Scottish communion. Thus my argument is that evangelical Christianity in 1801 was much more sacramental than it would soon become, even as it was spawning new rituals, rituals that were presumably more congruent with the vital experience of Christians. The easy task for the historian is to identify the new forms; the difficult one is to identify the exact qualities of experience they expressed.

Because it is a doctrinal and salvationist religion, Christianity, in all its forms, has always demanded proper conduct. It has endorsed moral standards. In this sense, it is incurably political. To be a Christian, an individual has to accept certain communal constraints within the church and assume a proper stance toward the outside world. At times of revival or renewal, almost by definition, all Christian confessions move closer to total dedication, to more inclusive or rigorous moral standards, to tighter or even more totalitarian forms of communal life, and either to a greater separation from the surrounding and sinful world, or to a more prophetic effort to convert or reform that world. The main distinctions among Christians, respecting their relationship to the larger society, involve this "either/or"—the position a given Christian sect chooses on a continuum from quietism or separation or retreat, at one extreme, to prophetic denunciation or radical reform at the other. But note that even the most separated sects, such as the Shakers, the Home Amish, the Hutterites, or the Old Colony Mennonites, are in a sense the most communal and totalitarian. They deny not only any proper separation, but any distinction, between the self and the community. Also, such separating communities, by their very demanding way of life, may bear a witness to the larger society that can at times be as powerful, as prophetic, as the legislative crusades of latter-day puritans who want to whitewash this old world and make it as righteous as possible.

Given these distinctions, the social implications of the revivals of 1801 make better sense. Because of deeply rooted cultural habits, tied to British origins and Calvinist doctrines, most of the people who gathered at Cane Ridge were not susceptible to quietism. It was not a live option. They were already too much involved with the world. The revival was therefore marked by an intensification of church discipline aiming toward greater moral purity, and by an increased effort to ameliorate what evangelicals saw as the prevailing evils of the larger society. In both cases, the churches became more rigorous and more repressive, at least from an outsider's perspective. During the great communions in Presbyterian congregations, the minister and Session tried, with greater zeal than ever before, to protect members from contamination by worldly vices—dancing, theater, horse racing, gambling, fancy or fashionable dress, card playing; to arbitrate and settle quarrels and jealousies among members; and to wean members away from improper love of wealth, speculative gains, or entrepreneurial success.

Being incurably political, these same evangelicals also tried to gain support for new legislation to emancipate slaves, to preserve the sanctity of the day of worship, and to outlaw vices. To gauge their degrees of political involvement, one must measure them by their standards, by what they considered the greatest evils in the larger society. In a very loose way, one can argue that the Presbyterians in the West, like the Congregationalists in New England, were both more actively involved, and perhaps because of educational or class differences, more effective than Baptists or Methodists in the political arena. Among some Baptists (a label that covers a broad spectrum of doctrines and religious cultures) and an even larger share of the early Disciples, one can identify quietist, separatist congregations, whereas the Methodists were never as politically active as good Calvinists.

One effect of revivals, often a divisive one, was a heightened sense of social equality. Equality within the church is of course a Christian imperative, but one whose exact implications have historically divided churches. Whatever the distinctions, subordinating or not, in the larger society, all Christians are supposed to be spiritual equals. Neither ethnicity, race, sex, social status, nor wealth is supposed to count within the kingdom. In fact, a high social status and great wealth are in theory an impediment to sainthood. The revivals of 1801 moved Christians back toward such egalitarian sentiments. The lowered class, racial, and gender barriers in turn explain much of the opposition to the more fervent revivals. At Cane Ridge, and subsequently among the New Lights, all traditional forms of authority and public deference seemed to erode. Traditional Presbyterians like David Rice, who very much yearned for a revival, were horrified when slaves or women began exhorting as equals, or when McNemar attacked ministerial prerogatives. The Shakers illustrated, in the clearest colors, the full implications of Christian equality—shared ownership, a lay ministry, the full equality of blacks, and at least in the early years the equal status of women. After all, a woman had founded the movement, and at the turn of the century another woman, Lucy Wright, was its acknowledged leader. This sexual equality represented one appeal of the Shakers. By every count, women made up a majority of members in all the evangelical churches.

The social equality supported by revivals raises several endlessly debated questions about blacks and about evangelical religion in the South. What we can know of the great revivals is insufficient to answer any of these questions, but suggests possible answers. Blacks in Kentucky, as in the Carolinas, joined Presbyterian churches as acknowledged spiritual equals. They shared the communion table with whites, as they did at Cane Ridge. Baptists and Methodists affirmed the same spiritual equality, and in these denominations this equality meant more, for in parts of the South blacks, a few free but most slaves, made up a majority of their members, something rarely if ever true among Presbyterians. Even by 1801, under white sponsorship or supervision, separate black Baptist and Methodist congregations met in several areas of the South, including Lexington. A developing form of black Christianity was thus a direct offspring of white evangelicalism. First the Virginia and Carolina Presbyterians, then Baptists and Methodists had conducted a very successful mission to slaves. The warm, evangelical style of Christianity appealed to blacks, apparently because it closely related to survivals of by then half-forgotten African religions. From the mid-eighteenth century on, the story of evangelical Christianity in the South was a story of both blacks and whites, of a wide expanse of shared beliefs, experiences, forms of baptism, testimonials, hymns, and even styles of preaching and congregational responses. But from the first conversions of blacks, cultural differences gave a distinctive black flavor to religion within each denomination.[2]

2. It is not my purpose to arbitrate the ongoing scholarly debate over black religion in the South. This debate continues, in part incited by two powerful books: Albert J. Raboteau, *Slave Religion: The "Invisible Institution" in the Antebellum South* (New York: Oxford University Press, 1978); and Eugene Genovese, *Roll, Jordon, Roll: The World the Slaves Made* (New York: Pantheon Books, 1974). The interracial aspects of southern evangelicalism is now a

This leads to ecstatic experience. Revivals featured a hot religion. The type or quality of experience became definitive. The word *revival* came to mean not just renewed commitment but an intensely affectionate form of religion. It meant a taste for ecstasy. The physical exercises at Cane Ridge illustrated the depth of feeling possible within Christianity. For those affected, the Spirit of God moved through the thickets and cane brakes with wondrous effects. The third person of the Trinity took precedence. People felt the power and received the gifts of the Holy Spirit. They did not always express that power in traditional ways, in large part because they knew little of earlier charismatic forms of Christianity. To many, what happened was nothing less than miraculous—the falling, the wisdom from the mouths of babes, or more magical, the people who remained in comas for days with no ill effects (the widely publicized record was nine days). As far as the records indicate, no one claimed the power of healing at Cane Ridge, and the forms of "miraculous" speech, the holy laughter or sounds from deep within the body, took a form other than glossolalia.

At least among the Shakers, glossolalia, prophecy, and healing became common, along with trances and visions. Since some individuals seemed more open to such trances, leadership often devolved upon the most charismatic individuals, those in a sense possessed by spirits, as in the case of such shamanlike leaders as Mother Ann Lee. These, of course, mark the extremes of charismatic religion. What was more enduring was what predominated at Cane Ridge—a tearful yet joyful religion that supported self-transcending types of experience most often expressed in audible prayers, in personal testimonies, in moving exhortations, in audience responses to sermons, and perhaps above all in song.

---

much studied phenomenon, with some of the very local returns published in John B. Boles, ed., *Masters and Slaves in the House of the Lord: Race and Religion in the American South, 1740–1870* (Lexington: University Press of Kentucky, 1988).

It was in the most experiential aspects of evangelical Protestantism that white and black cultures met and blended in ways that will be forever impossible to document. The blending began in Virginia and the Carolinas in the 1740s. Blacks, as they first responded to the proselytizing efforts of New Side Presbyterians, assimilated as much of the white religion as they could, fitting it to the shadowy survivals of African religions such as the circle shout (a form of dance) so often remarked, or condemned, by white masters. An older religious heritage, keyed to ecstatic experience, mixed with an especially experiential version of Christianity, one that already had precedents for shouting, for congregational responses, for spirited singing (but as yet without musical accompaniment), and on occasion an exhortatory pulpit style that could easily meld into incantations or chants.

By Cane Ridge, blacks were fully included yet preferred their own separate assemblies. They listened to their own ministers. Unfortunately, no witness left a detailed description of their services at the Cane Ridge sacrament. It is doubtful if they varied much from the white services, and in any case they would hardly have been more animated. In the subsequent Carolina union services, where blacks often made up half the crowd, they apparently did not hold separate services and seemed to experience the same exercises, and in the same proportion, as whites. At Cane Ridge, as John Lyle recorded in his diary, white ministers addressed the Negro assembly as a matter of respect and out of concern for their welfare. Yet blacks were not social equals, as concretely symbolized by the gallery in the Cane Ridge meetinghouse. Undoubtedly, almost all whites considered them in some sense inferior. White ministers treated them as children in the faith, less knowledgeable than most whites but not necessarily less pious. In fact, they sometimes seemed more affected and more devout, allowing ministers to use examples of the "poor Negroes" to inspire whites. As far as one can tell, whites often treated blacks in a condescending way but not as less than spiritual equals. They knew that their God did not elect people to salvation on the basis of either native intelligence or education.

The revivals hastened the conversion of blacks to Christianity and fostered a syncretistic mixing of Western and elusive African elements in black Christianity. What scholars will never agree on is the ratio of each in the mixture. The product was a distinctive form of Christianity, with the distinction being ethnic and not doctrinal, for despite the wide variations in black Christianity, certain common elements seemed present in most black churches. To specify these elements is the difficult task. That ethnic elements shaped black evangelicalism is not to make it more, or less, Christian. Ethnic elements are present in all varieties of Christianity. And all Western, Caucasian expressions of Christianity share a wide array of early borrowings from what Christians call pagan religions. It is not that no one is able to find the "pure" product but that the label has no content. The new black religion was as Christian as any other so long as blacks kept at the center of their religion a belief in Jesus as the liberating Messiah, a belief in salvation based on faith in this Messiah, and a devotion to the church as the medium of salvation, however distinctive their worship or their music. But blacks could, in later attempts to reclaim lost African roots, clearly move outside Christian limits, as in the Black Muslim movement. And, in a dozen later black cults, they could probe the outer boundaries of Christianity.

At Cane Ridge, Christians had to deal with slavery, not yet with the problems of the South. People at Cane Ridge were quite aware that they were in the West (this sensibility was a vital part of their identity), but were not in any self-conscious sense southerners. In many respects, the South of the later sectional conflict had yet to be born. In any case, central Kentucky was a middle area, never clearly a part of a South except that it was in an area with slaves. Such were the paths of migration, and of ministerial influence, that Cane Ridge had greater influence on Ohio than any state other than Kentucky. Both schismatic denominations that grew out of the revivals would remain strongest in middle areas—from southern Illinois, Indiana, and Ohio into Kentucky and Tennessee, and then in the areas to the west settled by such middle Americans, particularly Missouri and Texas.

Such qualifications should not obscure the effect of the Kentucky revivals east of the Appalachians, particularly in parts of the Old South. In a sense, the earlier religious influences that had flowed to the west were now reversed. In time, the warm and communal type of Christianity that probed the boundaries of both ecstasy and propriety at Cane Ridge would predominate all over the South, however broadly or narrowly one defines it. Up to 90 percent of Christians in the South, black or white, would be Methodists, Baptists, or Presbyterians, most with a decidedly evangelical flavor. The reasons for this dominance are several—the ethnic composition of early settlers, the numerical strength of blacks in the religious population, the effects of slavery on later migration routes, the energy and proselytizing tactics of these three denominations—but not, as often believed, southern ignorance or backwardness. Until waves of non-British immigration arrived in the mid-nineteenth century, the same denominations, plus Congregationalists, were almost as dominant in the North, particularly in the present Midwest. The South did not start out uniquely evangelical (to some extent it was less so), but in time it became such. And even though evangelicals monopolized southern religion, this does not mean that an evangelical culture ever gained full ascendancy in the South. It competed not so much with different forms of Christianity as with several very traditional and very resistant cultural norms that were non-Christian.

Although not yet burdened with the problems of the South, Christians at Cane Ridge had long struggled with the slavery issue. The revivals not only abetted egalitarianism, but briefly reinforced evangelical guilt over slavery. In Kentucky, almost as a rule, the more fervent supporters of revival took a stronger stand against slavery, while the anti-revivalists, with some notable exceptions, effected an earlier accommodation with the institution. As Donald G. Mathews has argued so persuasively, the turn of the century would be the last moment when southern evangelicals could still speak out for emancipation, as did Stone and his Cane Ridge congregation.[3] On this issue Presbyterians had already compromised more than Methodists. In Kentucky several Presbyterian ministers owned slaves, and one minister, notably not a leader in the revivals, stood accused before presbytery of cruelly whipping a female slave. In the soon inflamed sectional controversy, southern evangelicals slowly, painfully, guiltily retreated from even gradual emancipation to colonization to various rationalizations of what they hoped was an ameliorated form of slavery. In fact, if one attends to their language, they never really sanctioned slavery so much as, by verbal alacrity, they abolished it. That is, in order to make their peace with slavery, evangelicals tried to pull from it all its moral stigma by trying to convert and instruct slaves, by trying to convert and reform masters, and by trying to turn the plantation into a form of extended and supportive family. They turned slaves into beloved servants. This is a long, complex, and troubling story, but one as yet unanticipated at Cane Ridge, where for a brief moment even a glorious millennium seemed imminent.

Perhaps it is appropriate to end this story of Cane Ridge with an emphasis on religious experience. For those who yielded to the religious purposes of the great communion at Cane Ridge, the few days on the grounds turned out to be a mountaintop experience, ever memorable. For a brief while people forgot about all the ordinary concerns of an often hard life. Several even became so engrossed in the religious meaning of the event that they forgot to prepare meals or eat for two or three days. It may be hard for people today, except present evangelicals, to understand such behavior.

3. *Religion in the Old South* (Chicago: University of Chicago Press, 1977).

Memory helps. Once, as a child, I heard my grandfather report on a trip to a Methodist camp meeting, the last anywhere in my area of the country, and one that was only an attenuated shell of what such camps had once been. He said that it had been great fun. To me, it seemed inappropriate, even a bit blasphemous, to describe anything religious as fun. Now I think I understand. The people who had attended this old camp were those who could still shout praises or even leap for joy—those who could "get happy," as my grandfather put it. Such "exercises" were by then rare among Methodists or Presbyterians, and were indulged in largely by old people.

This memory reminds me of an obvious truth, one emphasized by John Dewey. The only justifying end of anything one does has to be, for someone, a good experience, something good in itself and not because it contributes to something else. All religions appeal to people because they promise just such self-justifying experience, proximate or remote. They all promise to enhance life, to give it meaning, to raise it to a new dimension. In their own distinctive ways, evangelical Christians tried to make good on this promise. They asked converts to probe the depths of despair and desolation, but only as the necessary down payment on inexpressible joy, both in the present and in the future. Such a warm religion enabled humble people, whose lives were so much more insecure and cruel than our own, to have fun. That was not a mean achievement.

Index

Index